D1085207

THE INTERLINGUAL CRITIC

THE
INTERLINGUAL
CRITIC

Interpreting Chinese Poetry

JAMES J. Y. LIU

Indiana University Press

Bloomington

Manufactured in the United States of America

Library of Congress Cataloging in Publication Data
Liu, James J. Y.
  The interlingual critic.
  Bibliography: p.
  Includes index.
  1. Chinese poetry—History—Criticism. 2. Criticism.
I. Title.
PL2307.L572   895.1'1'009   81-47010
ISBN 0-253-33030-0   AACR2
1 2 3 4 5 86 85 84 83 82

Contents

Preface   vii

Introduction   ix

1. *The Tetradic Circle*   1

2. *The Critic as Reader*   16

3. *The Critic as Translator*   37

4. *The Critic as Interpreter*   50

5. *The Critic as Arbiter*   65

6. *A Critical Exercise*   77

Epilogue   104

Notes   109

Bibliography   119

List of Chinese Words and Names   125

Index   128

Preface

THIS BOOK CONTAINS elements of polemics, autobiography, theory of literature, phenomenology of reading, theory of translation, hermeneutics, poetics, and practical criticism. However, it has a definite focus: the critical interpretation and evaluation of Chinese poetry for English-speaking readers. It is intended to raise questions rather than to solve them, to provoke discussion rather than to invoke dogma. I could have written a much longer book but have chosen to be as concise as possible, because long books on academic subjects are both boring and expensive. I have always believed that one who throws stones should not live in a glass house; whether the house I have just built is made of glass, only time can tell. Meanwhile, I fully expect stones to be thrown at me from all directions, but I make no promise to retaliate every shot.

All Chinese words and names are romanized according to the *pinyin* system, except for those that have long been naturalized, such as Confucius, Taoism, and Peking. It seems to me that to insist on writing "Beijing" instead of "Peking" is like insisting on writing "Firenze" instead of "Florence" and "München" instead of "Munich." Also, if persons and institutions have their own preferred forms of romanization, these have not been changed. Thus, "Tsing Hua University," "Fu Jen University" (as they were known in my time in Peking), and "Shuen-fu Lin," rather than "Qinghua University," "Furen University," and "Lin Shunfu." When quoting Chinese poems or lines of verse, I first give the original text, then the romanization accompanied by a word-for-word translation, and finally a more intelligible English version, which does not pretend to be English poetry. All other Chinese words, phrases, and names mentioned in the text are given in the List of Chinese Words and Names, arranged in alphabetical order according to the *pinyin* romanization, with the Wade-Giles romanization in brackets, and the Chinese characters. I hope this may help readers not familiar with the *pinyin* but familiar with the Wade-Giles system. Chinese characters that appear only in the notes or the bibliography are not included in the list.

Some of the material in the introduction and in chapter 1 has previously appeared in "Towards a Synthesis of Chinese and Western Theories of Literature," *Journal of Chinese Philosophy*, Vol. 4 (1977); parts of chapter 3 have appeared in "Polarity of Aims and Methods: Naturalization or Barbarization?" *Yearbook of Comparative and General Literature*, No. 24 (1975) and in "Language—Literature—Translation: A Bifocal Approach in a Tetradic Framework," in T. C. Lai, ed., *The Art and Profession of Translation* (Hong

Kong, n.d.); chapter 6 is substantially reprinted from "Time, Space, and Self in Chinese Poetry," *Chinese Literature: Essays, Articles, Reviews*, Vol. I, No. 2 (1979). However, this book is not a mélange of previously published and hitherto unpublished articles, but an attempt to weave various strands of thought into a coherent pattern.

I wish to acknowledge with thanks a National Endowment for the Humanities Fellowship, which enabled me to write this book during my sabbatical year 1978–79, and a grant from the Center for East Asian Studies, Stanford University, to cover the cost of typing the manuscript.

INTRODUCTION

DURING THE PAST two decades or so, an increasing number of books, articles, dissertations, and papers have appeared in English, all of which purport to be, implicitly if not explicitly, critical studies of Chinese poetry. Who are the people who write these works? Why do they write? And for whom do they write? Simple and obvious as these questions may be, they have seldom been raised, let alone answered. Let me try to answer them as briefly and bluntly as possible, before proceeding to consider in greater detail some of the implications of my answers. Roughly speaking, there are two kinds of critics who write in English about Chinese poetry: native speakers of Chinese (no matter what dialect) who were born and educated in China but are now living in an English-speaking country or at least working at an academic institution where the medium of instruction is English, and native speakers of English or some other European language who have studied Chinese as an academic subject and are engaged professionally in teaching or studying Chinese literature. Of course, there may be some cases in between, such as those who speak some Chinese dialect as their first language but have been educated mostly in English, and those whose native language is English but have lived for years in China. The relative advantages and disadvantages of these two kinds of interlingual critics will be discussed later. For the time being, let us simply register their existence.

As to why they write, a cynic might reply that since practically all those who write about Chinese poetry are academics, they are expected to write and publish, or perish. But apart from practical motives, I believe that most people who write about Chinese poetry genuinely wish to accomplish something intellectually meaningful to themselves and their readers, although their intellectual aims are not always clearly defined.

The question "For whom do they write?" is also often left unanswered. Some writers appear to address other specialists, for they make liberal use of Chinese words, names, and book titles without any explanation or translation, and refer frequently to Chinese works that the reader is presumed to be able to consult. In that case, one wonders why such a reader would need English translations of Chinese poems. If, on the other hand, the critical works are intended for readers who do not know Chinese, then the transliterated but unexplained Chinese words, names, and book titles would be meaningless, and the references to Chinese works useless. I do not mean to suggest that it is impossible to write for more than one kind of reader, but only point out the necessity of making some simple technical adjustments, such as relegating specialized discussions to footnotes and separating works in Chinese from those in Western languages in the bibliography.

There are, I realize, some Western scholars who think that writings in English about Chinese poetry should be limited to translation and annotation but should not attempt criticism. Such modesty is commendable but cannot fully absolve one from the onerous responsibilities of interpretation and evaluation, which together constitute practical criticism, since translation is a form of interpretation, though neither necessary (except in an interlingual situation) nor sufficient, and the choice of poems to translate implies prior value judgment, even if this is not independently arrived at but inherited from native critics. Individuals, of course, have the right to limit themselves to translation and annotation, but this should not prevent others from attempting overt interpretation and evaluation.

If interpretation and evaluation are the main tasks of a critic, whether practicing interlingual or intralingual criticism, then problems involved in interpreting and evaluating Chinese poetry for the benefit of English-speaking readers obviously deserve serious attention, yet these problems have seldom been squarely faced. Furthermore, anyone who writes about poetry must have some conception of what it is, as well as some idea as to how one should study it and what one may hope to achieve by studying it, yet few writers on Chinese poetry have explicitly stated their basic conceptions of poetry or their critical approaches. Some have borrowed terms, concepts, methods, and standards from one school of modern Western criticism or another, with or without acknowledgment, and have used such words as "archetype" and "intertextuality" without closely examining their precise meanings or considering the degree of their applicability to Chinese poetry.

Similarly, the most elaborate but jejune kind of semiotic analysis has been applied to the simplest kind of anonymous Chinese poetry, with impressive diagrams and charts but little real insight.

While I do not approve of indiscriminate application of modern Western critical terms, concepts, methods, and standards to Chinese poetry, I cannot agree with those who go to the opposite extreme of insisting that one should only adopt a traditional Chinese approach to Chinese poetry, for several reasons. To begin with, traditional Chinese criticism does not represent a single approach but involves various concepts of poetry, as I have attempted to show elsewhere.[1] Indeed, I have stressed the diversity in traditional Chinese thinking about literature, and it seems to me that those scholars who wish to paint a monolithic picture of "the Chinese view of literature" betray the same kind of mentality that created such popular myths as that all Chinese look alike. Second, traditional Chinese critical terms and concepts themselves require interpretation before they can be used in English. Third, traditional Chinese critics wrote for an elite readership with shared educational and cultural backgrounds, so that they took much for granted and felt no need to define their terms or identify their references, whereas a critic writing in English can take little for granted. Even someone writing in Chinese today can hardly assume that the reader is familiar with the whole tradition of classical Chinese literature. Fourth, the very fact that one is writing in English makes the interlingual critic a comparativist, willy-nilly. As soon as one uses the word "poetry," one is assuming that there is something in common between what is called "poetry" in English and what is called *shi* in Chinese. Here we are already running into trouble, for there are other Chinese literary genres such as *ci*, *qu*, and *fu*, which may or may not be considered "poetry," but I will not pursue the problem here.

Indeed, there are more positive reasons for adopting a comparative approach. As George Steiner has rightly observed, "literature should be taught and interpreted in a comparative way," and "chauvinism . . . has no place in literature."[2] A comparative approach to Chinese poetry will help avoid cultural chauvinism and parochialism not only by making students of Chinese poetry aware of other poetic and critical traditions but also by making students of Western poetry aware of Chinese poetry and poetics. At the same time, such an approach will also enable one to view Chinese poetry in a broader perspective and throw new light on it, for it is often by comparison that one becomes aware of the distinctive if not unique features and qualities of poetry in a particular language. A Chinese critic without knowledge of any other language, for example, may not realize that tonal patterns are a distinctive feature of Chinese poetry.

Since I have raised the three questions of *who*, *why*, and *for whom* at the beginning, it seems only fair that I should answer them with regard to myself. I shall first explain my linguistic, educational, and intellectual backgrounds, and then state my present aims and specify the kinds of readers for whom I am writing. What follows is not so much an *apologia pro vita sua* as a case history of "the making of an interlingual critic," which may interest readers curious to know how I came to write in English about Chinese poetry.

I was born in Peking and lived there for the first twenty-two years of my life. My father was a traditional Confucian gentleman, who in his younger days published translations in classical Chinese of some English short stories and one detective novel, but I never heard him speak English. His interest in serious English literature can be gauged by the fact that when he read Leslie Hotson's *The Death of Marlowe*, which for the first time correctly identified Marlowe's killer as Ingram Frizer, he thought it worthwhile to make a note of it in his diary, as I discovered years later. On his bookshelves were some books and periodicals in English, into which I peered out of curiosity. It was among the pages of *The Bookman* (or was it *The Century* or *The American Mercury*?) that I first saw photographs of some American and British authors, whom I later identified as Henry James, Joseph Conrad, Virginia Woolf, and others. Little did my father dream that years after his death his youngest son would write academic theses on Woolf and Marlowe.

The primary school that I attended was a modern one, and the curriculum did not differ radically from that of an American elementary school. However, during summer vacations my mother made me memorize some Confucian classics, such as the Four Books (*The Analects of Confucius*, *The Book of Mencius*, *The Great Learning*, and *The Doctrine of the Mean*) as well as some Tang poetry. Some of the classics had notes and paraphrases in modern Chinese, so that they were more or less comprehensible. Even if I did not fully understand everything I memorized, the experience proved very valuable later, for it is a great advantage to recognize quotations and sources of allusions when reading classical Chinese. As for the Tang poems, I enjoyed reciting them, and wrote my first juvenile "poem," a pentasyllabic Quatrain (*jueju*) when I was seven. For reasons I need not go into, I went to five different middle schools (which corresponded to American junior and senior high schools) and finished in five years instead of the usual six by skipping the third year of junior middle school. Most of the schools I attended emphasized science and mathematics, but we did have to memorize quite a number of classical Chinese texts, both prose and verse, and it was in junior middle school that I first wrote essays in classical Chinese. As for foreign languages, when I was in primary and middle schools, Japanese was a compulsory subject, Peking then being under Japanese occupation, but out of resentment we managed to forget most of what we had learned at the end of each academic year, so that after eight years I still did not master the Japanese language. I began formal study of English in the first year of junior middle school (previously I had picked up a few words of English from my elder sisters and brothers) and continued for five years, under various teachers, some Chinese, others English, and one Spanish. It was the Spanish teacher of English who lent me the first book in English I ever read from cover to cover apart from school textbooks: Thackeray's *The Book of Snobs*, of all things! To improve my English, I took private lessons from an Oxford-educated Englishwoman and mixed socially with other English people. I also took French lessons, first from a Chinese Catholic priest, who spoke with a Marseillaise accent, then with a Dutch priest, who spoke with a Dutch accent. On my own, I read various works including those of Tolstoy, Turgenev, Dostoevsky, and Gorky in Chinese translation, and those of Dickens, Hardy, and Wilde in English. By the time I graduated from senior middle school, I could read English without much difficulty and speak and write grammatical English.

At Fu Jen University, also known then as the Catholic University of Peking, I majored in Western Languages and Literature and took a variety of courses from a truly cosmopolitan faculty. To give just a few examples: I studied English and American literature with Chinese and American professors, French language with two Chinese professors (one of whom spoke with a Parisian accent and made me unlearn my Marseillaise and Dutch accents; the other had a strong Henan accent),

Latin with a German priest who conducted his classes in English and taught us the pronunciation of Church Latin with its Italian propensities, so that we pronounced "Caesar" more like "Chase-her" than "Seize-her," French literature with a French Sinologist, and Greek and Roman literature in English translation with a German professor, Gustav Ecke, who was well known in the West as an authority on Chinese art. How I survived, linguistically, such a curiously mixed education (which at the time did not strike me as such) is a mystery to me. At the same time, we had to take courses in Chinese history and literature and to write essays in classical Chinese, using a brush and not a pen. Apart from authors we studied in class, I discovered William Blake on my own, from some books left to my family for safekeeping by an English friend who was being sent by the Japanese to a concentration camp in Weixian, Shandong province. It was one of the most exciting experiences of my intellectual life. Eventually I took my B.A. with a thesis written in English on Virginia Woolf, having read all her novels and some of her essays, as well as the few critical studies of her works then available. It was long before she became a popular cult, and books by her and about her were not easy to obtain in China. I managed to get a Chinese pirated edition of *Mrs. Dalloway*, a Japanese edition of *To the Lighthouse* with notes in Japanese, and a Tauchnitz paperback edition of *Orlando*. The rest I borrowed from the National Peking Library, university libraries, and friends. Meanwhile, I had published some translations, including an early poem by T. S. Eliot, a fairy tale by Oscar Wilde, and a short story by Katherine Mansfield.

I then entered the graduate school of National Tsing Hua University and continued to study English literature, including Chaucer, Shakespeare, Donne, and modern poetry, as well as French literature. Sir William Empson was then teaching at both Tsing Hua and Beida (short for Beijing Daxue or Peking University), and I attended his lectures on Shakespeare and modern poetry at both universities. I also struggled through his *Seven Types of Ambiguity*, even though he had warned us to keep off it. After one semester at Tsing Hua I left for England, having been awarded a British Council scholarship. At the University of Bristol I began writing an M.A. thesis on Marlowe, under the supervision of Bertram L. Joseph, who made arrangements for me to be admitted to Wadham College, Oxford University, on the understanding that I would submit the thesis, when completed, to Bristol and not Oxford. The Warden of Wadham, Sir Maurice Bowra, having been born in China and being a comparativist, encouraged me to undertake comparative studies of Chinese and Western literature. My first efforts in this direction resulted in a paper, *Elizabethan and Yuan*, which was later published in London as a pamphlet.[3] I also published some translations of classical Chinese poetry and notes on Marlowe and Shakespeare.

Subsequently I taught Chinese at the School of Oriental and African Studies, University of London. During my five years in London I read a great deal of Chinese poetry as well as literature in English, including most of the novels of Henry James. I published a few of my own poems in modern Chinese and more translations of classical Chinese poetry.

Next I went to Hong Kong and taught first in the Chinese Department of Hong Kong University and then in the English Department of New Asia College, which became part of the Chinese University of Hong Kong. During my five years in Hong Kong I published articles and poems in classical Chinese, modern Chinese, and English. In fact, it was in Hong Kong that I wrote my first book, although it was not published until several years later, after I had come to the United States.

Since coming to the United States, I have taught Chinese literature at the universities of Hawaii, Pittsburgh, and Chicago, and at Stanford University. I have published six books and numerous articles on Chinese literature, some of which have been translated (or mistranslated, with or without permission) into Chinese (ironically enough), Japanese, and Korean. It is not that I can no longer write Chinese; I simply do not have the time to rewrite in Chinese everything that I have written in English. Besides, most of my works have been specifically intended for the Western reader. Apart from poetry, which I now prefer to write in classical Chinese, I am indifferent as to which language I use, Chinese or English, for most purposes. As far as English is concerned, I have had to make some adjustments in pronunciation, vocabulary, and spelling. I have learned to say "tomayto" instead of "tomahto," and "sidewalk" instead of "pavement" (otherwise I might have been run over by a "lorry"—I mean a "truck"), and publishers' copyeditors see to it that I write "color" instead of "colour," although

I notice that when American publishers publish works by English authors they do not insist on Americanizing the spelling or the vocabulary. But these linguistic readjustments have not been difficult.

Intellectually, I have naturally been influenced by various writers, both Chinese and Western. When I first sketched a theory of poetry as a double exploration of "worlds" and language in *The Art of Chinese Poetry*,[4] the theory was partly derived from certain traditional Chinese critics whom I then designated Intuitionalists—Yan Yu (fl. 1180–1235), Wang Fuzhi (1619–92), Wang Shizhen (1634–1711), and Wang Guowei (1877–1927)—and partly from such symbolist and post-symbolist poet-critics as Mallarmé and Eliot, while on the methodological level my treatment of Chinese poetry was influenced by I. A. Richards and William Empson. Subsequently I tried to develop and clarify this theory in an article, "Towards a Chinese Theory of Poetry,"[5] in which I referred, not necessarily with approval, to such diverse critics as R. G. Collingwood, I. A. Richards, René Wellek, G. Wilson Knight, and W. K. Wimsatt, Jr. Still later, when I was preparing my book on Chinese theories of literature, I began to read such phenomenologists as Husserl, Merleau-Ponty, Roman Ingarden, and Mikel Dufrenne, and was struck by the similarities between some of Ingarden's and Dufrenne's ideas about literature and some of my own. For example, when I wrote, "Each poem embodies a world of its own," which is "at once a reflection of the poet's external environment and an expression of his total consciousness,"[6] or when I wrote, "The poet explores the potentialities of language as he seeks to embody a world in the poem, and the reader, by following the development of the verbal structure of the poem, repeats the process and re-creates the world,"[7] I did not know that Ingarden and Dufrenne had expressed somewhat similar notions in their descriptions of the literary work of art. Further, when I wrote, "It seems to me that a poem, once written, has only a *potential* existence, until someone reads it and actualizes it, to a greater or lesser extent, according to that reader's ability to re-create the poem,"[8] I did not realize that Dufrenne had repeatedly maintained that a poem truly exists only when perceived by a reader and "consecrated" by that perception,[9] or that Ingarden, though strongly opposed to psychologism, had admitted that "every concretization [of a literary work of art] necessarily belongs to the corresponding subjective experiences and exists if, and only if, these experiences exist."[10] Again, when I suggested that it would be better to describe the structure of a poem as "polyphonic" rather than "stratified,"[11] I had no direct knowledge of Ingarden's theory of the stratified structure of the literary work of art but only Wellek's brief account of it, which, as I learned later, Ingarden repudiated as a misrepresentation,[12] nor was I aware that Ingarden himself had used the word "polyphonic," though with reference to what he called "aesthetic value qualities" rather than the structure of a work.

These similarities were not purely fortuitous coincidences, I realized, but (apart from any influences I may have felt indirectly from these theorists or earlier Western thinkers who had influenced them) may have stemmed from affinities between these Western theorists and certain Chinese critics, especially those whom I formerly called Intuitionalists but now prefer to call critics holding metaphysical views of literature, and from whom I had consciously or unconsciously derived some of my ideas. These affinities in turn may have stemmed from underlying philosophical affinities between phenomenology and Taoism, the latter of which profoundly influenced the Chinese critics concerned. What some of these affinities may be I have pointed out in *Chinese Theories of Literature*, and only a very brief summary need be given here.

In the first place, the Chinese metaphysical concept of literature as a manifestation of cosmic Tao is comparable to Dufrenne's concept of art as a manifestation of Being, and the Taoist concept of Tao itself is comparable to the phenomenological-existential concept of Being, such as expounded by Heidegger. Second, some Chinese critics who held metaphysical views of literature (even if they did not hold these exclusively) asserted the solidarity of *wo* ("I" or "subject") and *wu* ("thing" or "object") and the inseparability of *qing* ("feeling" or "inner experience") and *jing* ("scene" or "external environment"), just as some phenomenologists asserted the solidarity of "subject" and "object" and the inseparability of "noesis" and "noema." Third, both the Chinese critics influenced by Taoism and the phenomenologists advocate a kind of second intuition, which is attained after the suspension of judgment on reality. Finally, both groups recognize the paradoxical nature of language as an inadequate but necessary means to express the inexpressible and to rediscover the preconceptual and prelingual state of consciousness in which no distinction between subject and object exists.

Indeed, it is possible that the idea of the solidarity of "subject" and "object" was basic to traditional Chinese thinking, as suggested by some features of the classical Chinese language. For one thing, in classical Chinese there is no equivalent to "I am." The nearest counterpart is *you wo* or "There is I," which belongs to the same category of statements as "There is a tree," in contrast to the egocentric "I am." When anyone writing in a Western language wishes to avoid this egocentrism, he is forced to be ungrammatical, such as when Rimbaud says "Je *est* un autre." Strictly speaking, *you* means "have," but it would be absurd to take *you wo* as "Someone or something has me," instead of "There is I." Even in modern Chinese, the equivalent to "I am," *Wo shi*, usually requires a complement: one has to say, "*Wo shi* something." The expression *Wo cunzai* for "I am" or "I exist" was a neologism coined to translate "Cogito ergo sum." Furthermore, in classical Chinese the subject of a verb is often left unidentified, which suggests that traditional Chinese thinking was not teleologically but phenomenologically oriented. But to pursue this question further would be beyond the scope of the present book.[13]

I could no doubt think of other intellectual influences than those mentioned above, but I am less interested in influences than confluences, less in the phylogenesis of my ideas than their potentials for synthesis with other ideas. As an interlingual critic of Chinese literature, especially poetry, I have always aimed at a synthesis of Chinese and Western critical concepts, methods, and standards. My most recent effort in this direction was an article entitled "Towards a Synthesis of Chinese and Western Theories of Literature," which is partially reprinted in this book, since in order to provide the ensuing discussions with a conceptual framework and a theoretical basis, it is necessary to repeat the substance of what I wrote in the article.[14] I shall first set forth the theoretical framework and describe my basic conception of poetry formulated within that framework, then discuss some problems of reading, translation, interpretation, and evaluation, insofar as these affect the interlingual critic of Chinese poetry, and finally illustrate my own current approach to Chinese poetry with analyses of the interrelations between time, space, and self in some Chinese poems.

Although I am writing primarily for English-speaking readers of Chinese poetry, what I have to say may be applicable, *mutatis mutandis*, to other literary genres such as fiction and drama. Further, I hope that this book may be of some interest to students of comparative literature, general theories of literature, and hermeneutics. Since I am writing for several kinds of readers, it is necessary at times to explain what may seem obvious or elementary to some readers but not to others. For this I must ask for the indulgence of all readers.

THE INTERLINGUAL CRITIC

1

The Tetradic Circle

T HE CREATION of every work of art necessarily involves four elements: the world, the artist, the work, and the audience or spectator. The world consists of both the natural world and the cultural world in which every individual lives, and although no two individuals perceive and experience exactly the same world, we may posit one "world" for all, for without a common world no communication is possible. The interrelations among the four elements involved may be illustrated by the following diagram:

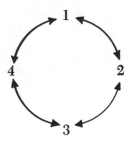

Here, 1 represents "world," 2 "artist," 3 "work of art," and 4 "audience" or "spectator." The world naturally affects the artist, who reacts to it, and this self-world interaction constitutes this artist's lived world or *Lebenswelt*. By exploring this lived world as well as other, possible worlds, the artist then creates an imaginary world in a work of art. When a spectator perceives the work of art, it will affect him in certain ways, and he will react to it in certain ways. Of course, he does not come to the work with a blank mind, but with all his previous experiences of the world and of art. After his experience of the work of art, his interaction with the world will be modified to some extent and in some ways. At the same time, by reacting to the work, the spectator comes into contact with the artist's mind and recaptures the latter's interaction with the world. That is why the arrows point in both directions in the diagram.[1]

The same tetradic circle can apply to every speech act, which necessarily involves the world, the speaker, language, and the hearer, for whenever something is said, the following conditions must be present: what is said must be about something (and the world is the sum total of "somethings" about each of which something can be said); there must be someone saying it; there must be some language to say it in; and there must be someone hearing it, even if it is the speaker himself, who cannot help hearing what he is saying. If we substitute "speaker" for "artist" at position 2, "language" for "work" at position 3, and "hearer" for "audience" at position 4, then the diagram will illustrate the situation of any speech act.

It should be obvious that the diagram will also apply to poetry, since poetry is both an art and a kind of speech act. The assumption that poetry is an art does not seem to need any justification. As for poetry as a speech act, I disagree with those who consider poetry to be an imitation of a speech act[2] or a quasi–speech act (shades of Aristotle!): for what basic difference is there between saying "I love you" orally and writing a love poem, or between writing a love poem to an actual person and writing one to an imaginary lover? Are Elizabeth Barrett's *Sonnets from the Portuguese* a more genuine speech act and therefore less poetic than Emily Brontë's "Cold in the earth—and the deep snow piled above thee" because the former were actually addressed to Robert Browning and the latter was addressed to a product of childhood fantasy? Nor do I find it particularly helpful to apply the Austinian distinctions between locutionary, illocutionary, and perlocutionary acts to poetry.[3] For one thing, it is often difficult to say what kind of illocutionary act a poet is performing in a given poem. For example, when Wang Wei (701–761?) writes,

明月松間照
清泉石上流

ming yue song jian zhao
bright moon pine amidst shine
qing quan shi shang liu
clear spring rock upon flow[4]

Bright moon shines among pines,
Clear spring flows over rocks,

what kind of illocutionary act is he performing? We could, I suppose, say that he is "describing," but for whose benefit, his own or ours? If it is for his own benefit, why should he find it necessary to tell himself in words, and in an antithetical couplet to boot, what he must have known perfectly well he was perceiving? If it is for our benefit, can we be sure that he had an audience in mind when he wrote the lines? In any case, to say that a poet is "describing" or "representing" the world or that he is "expressing an emotion" is not to say very much about a poem. As for any perlocutionary effects a poem may have, these are generally irrelevant to its artistic value. For my own part, rather than asking what kinds of illocutionary and perlocutionary acts poetry may perform, I would simply observe that poetry differs from other speech acts in function but shares with them the same linguistic structure (although the linguistic structure of every individual poem is unique in the sense of not being identical with that of any other poem), while it differs from other arts in structure, its medium being language, but shares with them the same basic function. In other words, poetry may be conceived of as the overlapping of linguistic structure and artistic function. This conception of poetry does not oblige us to maintain the distinction between "poetic language" and "ordinary language," a distinction that has recently been shown to be untenable,[5] nor does it force us to the unhappy conclusion that poetry does not exist.[6] According to this conception, "poetic language" is not a special kind of language with identifiable features, but simply language that fulfills the artistic function. (What this is will be discussed below.) At the same time, the fact that there has never been a perfect and universally accepted definition of "poetry" does not mean that poetry does not exist, for the same is true of many other words, such as "religion" and "cat."[7] What I am attempting is not a perfect definition of "poetry" but a heuristic hypothesis that may help us turn the hermeneutical circle into an open-ended spiral of infinite reinterpretations and revaluations. I shall elaborate on this point in chapter 4.

In saying that poetry is the overlapping of linguistic structure and artistic function, I do not imply that it cannot fulfil other (i.e., nonartistic) functions, such as moral, social, and political ones, which the author may have consciously intended his work to fulfil. However, these are not what make it a work of art, just as Shang bronzes or Greek vases may have fulfilled utilitarian functions as containers, but these are not what make them works of art. Conversely, a poet may not have been conscious of the artistic function of his work, but this should not prevent us from discussing it.

What, then, is the primary artistic function of poetry? This I conceive to be twofold: extension of reality through the creation (on the part of the poet) and re-creation (on the part of the reader) of imaginary worlds, and satisfaction of the creative impulse of both poet and reader. To elaborate this concept of the artistic function of poetry, we can now examine it in the framework of the tetradic circle, placing "poet" (or "author" or "writer") at position 2, "poem" (or "work") at position 3, and "reader" at position 4. The diagram will illustrate how the poet creates an imaginary world out of his own *Lebenswelt* (which is constituted by his interaction with the "real" world) as well as other, possible worlds, and how the reader re-creates the world of the poem and thus recaptures the poet's interaction with the world. It should be realized that the world of the poem, which does not exist and has never existed in the real world, exists first in the poet's consciousness and, once created, exists potentially outside time and space, to be re-created by the reader's consciousness. Therefore, the world that emerges from the linguistic structure of the poem is not the same as the author's *Lebenswelt*, which merely provides the *occasion* for the creation of a work:[8] it is his *Lebenswelt* fused with and transmuted by the creative experience. Whether the author's *Lebenswelt* is knowable to us is open to question, but we may assume its existence, just as we may assume the existence of another person's "being," even if it can never be fully known to us. In any case, if an author's *Lebenswelt* is indeed unknowable, it will render impossible the task of the biographer, not that of the critic, whose concern is with the created world of the work.

Since the world of the poem has never existed in the real world, it is an *extension* of reality. This statement differs from both Wang Guowei's and my own earlier opinions. Wang wrote, "There are some [poets] who create worlds [*jingjie*] and others who describe worlds. This is the origin of the distinction between Idealism and Realism."[9] I disagreed with this and suggested that it was not so much a distinction between Idealism and Realism as one between great and lesser poets.[10] However, I now believe that every poem that is a genuine work of art has its own created world, which is an extension of reality, just as every painting that is a genuine work of art has its own created world. Even an apple in a *trompe l'oeil* painting exists only in the imaginary world created by the artist, with its own dimensions of space and time, and not in the real world. It therefore constitutes an extension of the reality of apples or "appleness." Of course, the existence of the apple as part of the imaginary world of the painting is not to be confused with the physical existence of the paint on the canvas, any more than the existence of a tree or a person in a poem is to be confused with the physical existence of the print on the paper in the real world.

The concept of the created world of the literary work of art is nothing new. As M. H. Abrams has demonstrated, the concept of the poem as heterocosm originated in the eighteenth century and has become a commonplace in Western criticism.[11] However, what is being proposed here does not imply, as did the Romantic concept of the heterocosm, an analogy between God the Creator and the artist as creator. Rather, the word "created" is used in contradistinction to "made," the difference between the two having been clearly shown by R. G. Collingwood.[12] Thus, to speak of the poet as a creator does not mean "raising the function of art to the level of something divine or making the artist into a kind of God."[13] It is worthwhile comparing our concept of the created world with Roman Ingarden's "represented" or "portrayed" world (*dargestellte Welt*) and Mikel Dufrenne's concept of the world of the aesthetic object, as well as with some Chinese antecedents.

Ingarden's description of the world of the literary work of art at times betrays traces of the mimetic concept of art, such as when he speaks of the "representation function" (*Repräsentationfunktion*) of the "represented" or "portrayed" objects (*dargestellten Gegenstande*), or when he remarks, "persons 'appearing' in literary works do not merely carry such names as 'Julius Caesar', 'Wallenstein', 'Richard II', etc., but are also in a sense supposed to 'be' the persons who were once so called and who once actually existed."[14] To me, however, whether a character in a literary work is an authentic historical figure like Julius Caesar, or a shadowy semihistorical figure like Macbeth, or a purely fictitious character like David Copperfield, or even a fabulous creature like Ariel, is irrelevant to its artistic nature and value, just as whether the subject of a painting is an authentic historical figure like Henry VIII, or a shadowy semihistorical figure like Homer, or a purely fictitious character like Adonis, or even a fabulous creature like the dragon killed by St. George, is irrelevant to its artistic nature and value. I do not deny that our previous knowledge about a historical person will affect our response to the work in which he appears, but I think such knowledge is not indispensable. Even someone who has never heard of Julius Caesar will not fail to see the historical significance of his assassination from Shakespeare's play itself, and presumably Marlowe's audience had no knowledge of the historical Timur, nor Voltaire's of the historical "orphan of China." How far the portrayal of a historical person in a literary work resembles the real person (assuming, for the sake of argument, that this is knowable) is a question about its *historical* value, which is a separate question from that about its *artistic* value, just as how far a portrait is a "good likeness" of the sitter is a question about its practical or sentimental value, which is a separate question from that about its artistic value, even if we are in a position to know what the person portrayed did look like, which we seldom are. In brief, I believe that although the created world of a literary work of art bears a necessary but variable relation to the real world, its artistic nature and value do not depend on the degree to which it resembles the real world.

However, it seems that Ingarden's basic conception of literature is not really mimetic, for he states that in every literary work there is a "more or less determined background, which, along with the represented objects, constitutes *an* ontic sphere."[15] This "ontic sphere" appears to be similar to what Wang Guowei called *jingjie* and what I call the "created world" of a poem. Furthermore, Ingarden took pains to point out that the character of "reality" possessed by the "represented objects" is "not to be identified with the ontic character of truly existing real objects," and yet "it would obviously be a mistake to assert that the represented objects possess no character of reality at all or that perhaps they take on the character of another ontic mode (i.e., that of *ideal* existence)."[16] In plainer English, what is presented in a literary work is not "real" in the sense of actually existing, nor "unreal" in the sense of nonexisting, nor yet "ideal" in the sense of existing in some transcendent world. This seems to me much closer to the truth than Sartre's insistence on the unreality of aesthetic objects. Sartre's comparison of the experience of watching a play to that of dreaming is misleading,[17] because a play is sharable but a dream is not. Although Hamlet and Ophelia are not real people, anyone can see them in the play, but no one can see another's dream. If a dreamer can describe his dream so vividly as to make me feel as if I could see it, I still cannot share his dream but only his description of it, since I am in no position to know whether what he describes is the same as what he actually dreamed. The dreamer, or rather the teller of the dream, has in fact become an artist. That is why I speak of the created world of a poem as an extension of reality, not as unreality.

As for Dufrenne's concept of the world of the literary work of art, it is certainly not mimetic, for he remarks, "the writer strives not so much to describe or mimic a pre-existing world as to evoke a world re-created by him."[18] Further, he conceives the world of the aesthetic object as being constituted by the "represented world" (*monde représenté*) and the "expressed world" (*monde exprimé*), the latter being like the soul of the former, which is its body. In his account of the world of the aesthetic object, Dufrenne shows affinities with certain traditional Chinese critics. First, when he speaks of the "world atmosphere" (*atmosphère de monde*), which is "a certain quality which words cannot translate but which communicates itself in arousing a feeling,"[19] he reminds one of Chinese critics who speak of *qixiang*, which may be translated as "atmosphere." For example, Jiang Kui (ca. 1155–ca. 1221) remarked, "In general, poetry must have its own atmosphere [*qixiang*], countenance [*timian*], veins [*xuemo*], and tone [*yundu*]."[20] Yan Yu mentioned "atmosphere" as one of the five principles of poetry and praised ancient poetry for its atmosphere, which is integral, holistic, and not discernible in isolated lines.[21] Wang Guowei, who used *jingjie* or "world" as the key term in his criticism, occasionally also spoke of *qixiang* or "atmosphere."[22] Although he did not explain the relation between the two, it seems reasonable to infer that the "atmosphere" of a poem emanates from its "world," and that the former is an indescribable quality that characterizes the latter. Further, Dufrenne stresses the subjective aspect of the world of the aesthetic object. To him, the aesthetic object is a "quasi-subject," and it expresses a personal vision of the world, a *Weltanschauung*, which "is not a doctrine but rather the vital metaphysical elements in all men, their way of being in the world which reveals itself in a personality."[23] In somewhat similar fashion, some Chinese critics also stressed the personal mode of sensibility, which reveals itself in an ineffable tone in poetry. Thus, Jiang Kui said, "The poetry of each master has its own flavor [*fengwei*], just as each of the twenty-four modes of music has its own tone [*yunsheng*], which is where the music comes to rest."[24] Wang Shizhen, who quoted this remark with approval, advocated *shenyun* or "spirit and tone," which, as I suggested elsewhere, involves not only intuitive apprehension of reality and intuitive control over the artistic medium but also a personal tone.[25] However, we should realize that this personal mode of sensibility or artistic persona, which is inherent in the work, is not to be confused with the historical, empirical person who created it. Or, to use the terminology of Jacques Maritain, the "creative Self" is not to be confused with the "self-centered ego."[26] Therefore, when Dufrenne identifies the world of the aesthetic object with the world of the author, we should understand by the "world of the author" a reference to the world that the author has created in his work or works, not one to his actual *Lebenswelt*. It also seems advisable to make a distinction between the world of an individual work and the total world of an author's whole corpus, the latter being the conglomeration of all the individual works that he has created.

With regard to creativity, although this is not as often stressed in Chinese criticism as in Western criticism, we do find some expressions of a concept of creativity in Chinese poetry and criticism. For example, the poet and critic Lu Ji (261–303) described the process of writing as, inter alia,

課虛無以責有
叩寂寞而求音

ke xuwu yi ze you
tax emptiness and demand being

kou jimo er qiu yin
knock silence and seek sound

Tax non-being to demand being,
Knock on silence to seek sound.[27]

The "demonic" poet Li He (790–816), in praising his senior contemporaries Han Yu and Huangfu Shi, wrote,

筆補造化天無功

bi bu zao-hua tian wu gong
brush repair creation heaven no merit[28]

Their pens supplement creation: Heaven has no merit.

The critic Xie Zhen (1495–1575) echoed Lu Ji when he wrote,

Whenever we climb high and let our thoughts roam, we communicate with the ancients in spirit. [Our thoughts] reach far and near, and we feel sorrow or joy accordingly. These things give rise to one another in a chance manner, thereby causing forms to appear where there was no trace of anything, and echoes to be evoked where there was no sound.[29]

Similarly, the critic Ye Xie (1627–1703) wrote,

When a poet is touched by something and his inspiration rises, his ideas, words, and lines all come out of the blue: they all come into being from nothingness. He takes them from his mind wherever he finds them, and expresses them as "emotions" (*qing*), "scenes" (*jing*), and "events" (*shi*).[30]

To return to the artistic function of poetry from the author's point of view: the process of creating an imaginary world is one of verbalization, or verbal incarnation, which involves an exploration of the possibilities of language as an artistic medium and the creation of a unique verbal structure (unique in the sense, already indicated, of not being identical with the structure of any other poem, rather than that of possessing unique linguistic features, just as every individual is unique in the sense of not being identical with any other individual, rather than that of possessing unique physical or mental attributes). It is this process that, when successfully carried out, satisfies the author's creative impulse and fulfils the second part of the artistic function of poetry for the author. This creative impulse is distinct from any ulterior motive—social, political, moral, or monetary—that the author may have, for such motives cannot account for the choice of the artistic medium and are often absent in any case. Why does anyone want to write a poem, then? Perhaps we can answer this by reversing the answer, made famous by Sir Edmund Hillary, to the question why anyone should want to climb Mount Everest: "Because it is *not* there." It seems only natural that a human being should want to create something and to feel a special kind of satisfaction on seeing that what he has created is good. A child who has succeeded in drawing, for no particular reason, what it considers a perfect circle, feels the same kind of satisfaction that Leonardo da Vinci may be supposed to have felt when he finished painting the Mona Lisa, the differences in quality between the two "works" notwithstanding. Similarly, when a writer has created a verbal structure to his own satisfaction, the act will have fulfilled his creative impulse; whether the work has any artistic value depends, among other things, on whether it enables us to satisfy our creative impulse. This leads us to a consideration of the artistic function of poetry from the reader's point of view.

As already suggested, a literary work of art exists potentially and awaits actualization (or concretization, in Ingarden's terminology) by a reader, so that rather than saying, with Archibald MacLeish, "A poem should not mean, but be," perhaps we shoud say, "A poem should not be, but become." The process of a poem's becoming, from the reader's point of view, is paradoxically both a reversal and a revival of the creative process. Insofar as the reader re-creates a world from the verbal structure of a poem, the process is one of deverbalization, which is the reversal of verbalization, yet insofar as the reader follows the words that make up the verbal structure, reading is an approximate reenactment of writing. I say "approximate," since, obviously, the reader's experience cannot be literally identical with the writer's, yet the two must be similar. As John Dewey put it,

> For to perceive, a beholder must *create* his own experience. And his creation must include relations comparable to those which the original producer underwent. They are not the same in any literal sense. But with the perceiver, as with the artist, there must be an ordering of the elements of the whole that is in form, although not in details, the same as the process of organization the creator of the work consciously experienced.[31]

In re-creating the world that the author has created, the reader extends his own *Lebenswelt* and his perception of reality, and thus the poem fulfils the first part of its artistic function for the reader. Paul Ricoeur appears to be expressing similar ideas when he writes,

> For us, the world is the ensemble of references opened up by the texts. Thus, we speak about the "world" of Greece, not to designate any more what were the situations for those who lived them, but to designate the nonostensive references which outlive the effacement of the first and which henceforth are offered as possible modes of being, as symbolic dimensions of our being-in-the-world. For me, this is the reference of all literature: no longer the *Umwelt* of the ostensive references of dialogue, but the *Welt* projected by the nonostensive references of every text we have read, understood, and loved. To understand a text is at the same time to light up our own situation or, if you will, to interpolate among the predicates of our situation all the significations which make a *Welt* of our *Umwelt*. It is this enlarging of the *Umwelt* into the World that permits us to speak of references opened up by the text—it would be better to say the references *open up* the world.[32]

If I understand him correctly, the World or *Welt* of which he speaks is constituted by the individual worlds that we have re-created from all the literary works that we have read, understood, and loved, while the world re-created by each reader from an individual work is an instance of the realization of the possibilities opened up by its nonostensive references. A word of caution may be necessary here: the expression "open up" should not be taken too literally. A work will only "open up" a world to a competent reader actively responding to it; obviously, it will not open up any world to someone ignorant of the language in which it is written or someone who is a competent reader but is not being attentive. Epiphany will come only to the deserving.

The world re-created by the reader is not to be mistaken as the author's *Lebenswelt*, since the work no longer refers ostensively to the author's actual situation or environment but nonostensively to all similar situations that may possibly exist. Even if a work contains references to actual persons, events, places, dates, and so forth (and Chinese poems are particularly replete with such seemingly ostensive references), it cannot revive the actual situation that provided the occasion for the creation of the work. What it can do is to let us experience an imaginary world that resembles the original situation. Poetry is not a time machine that can bring the past back to life; it is, rather, a magic carpet that can transport us into a world that exists outside time. By transcending the author's actual situation at the time of writing, poetry escapes from time into timelessness.

This is not to say that poetry deals only with the universal, but that it reveals the universal through the particular, or, to adopt the distinction made by E. D. Hirsch, Jr., between "meaning" and "significance,"[33] that poetry transcends its local meaning and acquires universal significance. That is why I wrote elsewhere that "the world of a poem is the concrete embodiment and individualization of a theme,"[34] and also, perhaps, why a poem can be a "concrete universal," as described by W. K. Wimsatt, Jr.[35]

Just as the reader's experience of re-creating a work is similar to, but cannot be identical with, the author's experience of creating it, so is the world re-created by the reader similar to, but not identical with, the one created by the author, or at least the two cannot be proven to be identical. How far they overlap or intersect each other depends on various factors (apart from the question of how far the author has succeeded in creating a world in a verbal structure in the first place), such as the reader's linguistic competence, knowledge about the author's cultural world, sense of affinity with the author's temperament, and employment of one's powers of perception, imagination, understanding, and reflection. We shall have occasion to return to this question of overlapping or intersecting worlds later.

Let us now consider further the second part of the artistic function of poetry from the reader's point of view. When we read a poem, whether aloud or silently, we have to say to ourselves certain words, and no other, in a certain order, and no other. In so doing, we are repeating, to some extent, the author's experience of putting these particular words in this particular order. The possibility of revision does not affect the issue, since in that case we can be said to repeat the author's experience of writing the final version. When we finish reading, if it is a successful poem, we shall realize that these are just the right words in just the right order, and this realization will give us a feeling of satisfaction comparable to the author's feeling of satisfaction at finishing the poem and seeing that it was good. It is this feeling of satisfaction, together with the experience of repeating the author's creative experience, that fulfils the reader's creative impulse. This feeling of satisfaction is not necessarily "pleasure": even if a poem shocks us or horrifies us, we are still "satisfied" that the author has employed the right strategy to produce the desired effect, just as a judge is "satisfied" that the defendant did commit the crime, without taking pleasure in the fact. Moreover, when we feel shocked or horrified by a poem, the feeling is not the same as if what is described were actually taking place: to read about someone's death is not the same as actually seeing someone die. The psychological distance involved ensures our aesthetic satisfaction.

Some readers may doubt the statement that in reading we repeat the author's process of writing. That this is so can be shown from even the simplest sentences. When we read the sentence "I am cold," even if we do not say it aloud, in which case we say the words mentally, we are repeating the act of saying these words, and not merely receiving the "message" that someone was cold. In other words, to understand what is said we have to temporarily put ourselves in the speaker's position. If reading were indeed merely a matter of decoding a message— if, for example, reading the line "Shall I compare thee to a summer's day" merely gave us the message that Shakespeare wondered whether he should compare his love (Lord Southampton, perhaps?) to a summer's day—of what possible interest could such a message be to us? I think that we read, and enjoy reading, the line because, first, it enables us to enter the imaginary world of this sonnet and experience the *speaker's* (not necessarily the *author's*) state of mind when he is imagined as saying these words, and, second, it gives us a feeling of satisfaction to repeat these words that the *author* has placed there, and to realize that these are just the right words in just the right order. I do not mean that we enjoy the words purely for the beauty of their sound apart from their meaning; on the contrary, our satisfaction is partly due to the fact that the sound reinforces the meaning. For instance, the long vowels and diphthongs compel us to slow down, as if we (identifying with the speaker while we read) were trying to slow down the passing of time and make this short "summer's day" last a little longer. What I have just said is, of course, also true of Chinese poetry, as well as music and perhaps even some kinds of visual arts. The satisfaction we get from looking at Chinese calligraphy and some Chinese paintings is due primarily, I think, not to the spatial relations among the lines and brushstrokes but to the temporal experience of repeating in our mind the movement of the artist's brush. In short, I believe that aesthetic experience is a kind of creative experience by proxy: to read a love poem is not a substitute for being in love but an approximate substitute for writing a love poem, just as looking at a painting of apples is not a substitute for eating or even looking at apples but an approximate substitute for painting them.

Having considered the artistic function of poetry, we should, logically, turn our attention to its linguistic structure. However, I do not intend to discuss this in detail, for several reasons. First, our discussions so far have in fact involved some structural considerations, because the relationship between structure and function is a dialectical one: it is the linguistic structure of a poem that enables it to fulfil its artistic function (as well as any nonartistic functions it may also fulfil), and it is the artistic function, whether consciously intended by the author or not, that (together with any nonartistic functions it may also fulfil) determines its linguistic structure. Second, since the linguistic structure of each poem is unique, it is more profitable to discuss the linguistic structure of an individual poem in relation to its artistic function than to discuss the linguistic structure of all poetry in general terms. Finally, even if we do wish to do so, Roman Ingarden has described the structure of the literary work of art in such detail that it would be difficult to add much to his description or to do it full justice with a brief summary. I venture, nonetheless, to raise two questions about terminology, not to register disagreement but to avoid any misunderstandings that may arise from Ingarden's use of certain terms.

In the first place, Ingarden describes the structure of the literary work of art as a stratified one, consisting of four strata: the stratum of linguistic sound formations, the stratum of meaning units, the stratum of represented objects (or objects projected by the state of affairs, the intentional correlates of the sentences), and the stratum of schematized aspects (or aspects under which these objects appear in the work). The expression "stratified" could give the misleading impression that the structure of a literary work of art is a static one, when in fact it is really a dynamic one, the four strata (which I would prefer to call "elements") interacting simultaneously. Ingarden himself did discuss the temporal dimension of the literary work of art, but this aspect of his theory has often been overlooked. I still think the word "polyphonic" would be a better description that "stratified," *pace* the reviewer of one of my books, who thought it "a pretty metaphor but fairly useless as far as theory is concerned,"[36] especially, as Ingarden himself used it, although in a slightly different context, as mentioned before.

Second, it seems to me the "represented objects" and the "schematized aspects" do not belong to the linguistic structure of the work but rather to the created world that emerges from that structure. To be sure, Ingarden does not specify that the structure he describes is purely linguistic, but in the interest of greater clarity it may be better to speak of the "created objects" (rather than "represented objects") and the aspects under which they appear as supralinguistic elements, which are constitutive of the created world, rather than as strata of the linguistic structure.

The concept of poetry described above implies that a poem, as a literary work of art, is both referential and self-referential, both signifier (*signifiant*) and signified (*signifié*), both centrifugal and centripetal (in Northrop Frye's sense).[37] In other words, the linguistic structure of a poem both transcends itself and draws attention to itself. In transcending itself, it yields a created world, which is an extension of reality; in drawing attention to itself, it satisfies the creative impulse of both author and reader. This concept of poetry can be applied, with modifications, to fiction and drama, but in the following pages we shall confine our discussions to what is generally considered "poetry."

2

The Critic as Reader

E VERY CRITIC, whether intralingual or interlingual, plays a dual role, as reader and as author: vis-à-vis the original author, the critic is a reader, but vis-à-vis the critic's own reader, he assumes the position of the author and his critical work replaces the original work for the time being, while the world created by the original author in the work replaces the real world. Actually, the interrelations between world, author, work, and reader are more complex than suggested by the circular diagram, which has been offered merely for the sake of convenience. If we enquire further into these interrelations, we shall find that the real world (including both the natural world and the cultural world), the author's lived world, the world created by the author in the work, the world re-created by the reader, and the reader's lived world form a daisy chain of intersecting circles, which can never be proven to be identical yet must intersect each other in order for any communication to take place. The critic's task as reader is to try to increase the area of intersection between the created world of the work and the world that he is re-creating from the linguistic structure of the work. How far he will succeed depends, among other things, on how much he knows about the author's cultural world and how far his own lived world resembles that of the author's. This does not mean that only someone who has lived in the same cultural world as the author and has had the same experiences can successfully read a poem, since obviously even two brothers who had the same back-

16

ground may react differently to the same environment, but it remains true that a knowledge of the author's cultural world and a sympathetic understanding of his created world are both necessary for a successful reading of a poetic work.

Hence, to be a competent reader of Chinese poetry requires not only linguistic competence (knowledge of the vocabulary, syntax, phonology, and prosody of a given period and a given genre) and historical knowledge, but also the capacity to make the imaginative leap across temporal and spatial barriers into the world created by the author. Linguistic competence and historical knowledge are necessary but not sufficient conditions for a successful reading of poetry as something more than historical documents or linguistic data. (I am not repeating the old opposition between "reading literature as literature" and "reading literature as social documents," which John M. Ellis has shown to be a false opposition,[1] but asserting that poetry is something *more than* historical documents or linguistic data.) Moreover, just as a connoisseur of wine may choose to talk about the bouquet, color, body, and taste of a vintage wine rather than the soil and climate where the vine grew and the kind of fertilizer used, so may a critic choose to talk about the linguistic structure and aesthetic qualities of a poem rather than the circumstances in which the poet lived and wrote. One more consideration may be brought forward: the distinction between a literary historian and a literary critic. Although a literary historian should also have critical discernment and a critic should also have historical awareness, the concerns and methods of the two are not identical. The former is by definition committed to a diachronic view of literature; the latter may, and sometimes must, take a synchronic view, for otherwise it would be impossible to establish any critical standards that are not historically relative. We shall pursue the question of historical relativism further in chapter 4.

The question "Who is a competent reader?" is not as easy to answer as "Who is a competent speaker?" Whereas any normal adult speaker of a language can be presumed to be a competent speaker of that language, no simple criterion exists for competence as a reader of poetry. The question is a particularly sensitive one with regard to classical Chinese poetry, since many who write in English about Chinese poetry are not native speakers of Chinese, and some do not even speak any Chinese at all. Such people will probably argue that no one is a "native speaker" of classical Chinese. Although I do not deny this, I think it is legitimate and useful to distinguish "native readers" from "non-native readers." By a "native reader" of classical Chinese poetry I mean someone who was born and brought up in China, speaks some modern Chinese dialect as his native language, and has been reading and writing classical Chinese since childhood; by a "non-native reader" I mean someone whose native language is not Chinese and who has learned to read classical Chinese as an adult. (Those who fall into neither category may be considered "near-native" or "semi-native" readers, as the case may be.) Both kinds of readers can become competent readers of Chinese poetry, but each has certain advantages as well as disadvantages. Let us consider these.

The native reader naturally enjoys some advantages over the non-native reader, both linguistically and culturally. Linguistically, classical Chinese is, after all, not a totally different language from modern Chinese in any of its dialectal forms. I imagine no one would deny that a native speaker of Italian or French has a natural advantage over a native speaker of Chinese or Japanese when it comes to reading Latin, and I see no reason to pretend that a native speaker of modern Chinese does not enjoy a comparable advantage over a native speaker of an Indo-European language when it comes to reading classical Chinese. Since classical Chinese shares with modern Chinese the same script and, to some extent, the same vocabulary, though differing in syntax, a native speaker of modern Chinese is unlikely to make the kind of elementary mistake that a non-native reader may, such as taking Chijiao Daxian to mean "The Red-legged Immortal" instead of "The Bare-footed Immortal," as a famous English translator of Chinese literature did. Also, a native reader tends to respond intuitively to a poem as a whole, rather than trying to decode it word by word. Furthermore, a native reader is likely to be more sensitive to the rhythm and tonal patterns of Chinese poetry than a non-native reader, despite the differences between classical and modern Chinese in actual pronunciation. As for writing classical Chinese, some may argue that the kind of "classical Chinese" that a modern Chinese may write is not the same language that Du Fu wrote, but then Du Fu's classical Chinese is not the same language as that of the *Book of Poetry*, just as Milton's Latin is not the same as Vergil's. As long as a piece of writing follows the same basic semantic, syntactic, and, in the case of verse, prosodic rules as classical Chinese, it may be considered a work in classical Chinese, of whatever quality. The advantage of being used to writing classical Chinese and not merely reading it is that one acquires a feel for the medium and can appreciate the subtleties and difficulties of writing classical Chinese poetry, or what we call in Chinese the "sweetness and bitterness therein" (*qizhong ganku*), from the inside, as it were, just as someone who has been singing all his life, no matter what an indifferent singer he may be, is in a better position to appreciate good singing than someone who has never sung a note in his life, no matter how much he may know about music. Culturally, the native reader has the natural advantage of having lived in a cultural world somewhat closer to that of the classical Chinese poet than a non-native reader. Of course, modern China is not the same as ancient China, but the two still have more in common with each other than either with the Western world, past or present. For instance, to someone who grew up in Peking before the city walls were torn down, the word *cheng* would immediately convey the double meaning of "city wall" and "walled city," with definite visual connotations, which, to someone who grew up in Manhattan, may not be readily perceptible. The same is true of traditional beliefs, assumptions, legends, folklore, and so forth, which a native reader has assimilated unconsciously from childhood, but a non-native reader has to learn consciously.

The native reader of Chinese poetry also has certain disadvantages. To begin with, as a native speaker of modern Chinese he may easily assume that a word or phrase in classical Chinese means the same as in modern Chinese, which is often not the case. Therefore, he has to be constantly on guard against such assumptions and remind himself of the differences between classical and modern Chinese. Second, having been brought up on standard authors and works, his taste can easily be shaped by traditional standards, and it takes a conscious effort to form independent tastes and judgments. Finally, since he more or less knows "what there is" in Chinese poetry, there is little likelihood of discovering a poet or a work that he has never heard of before. Reading poetry for such a reader is a gradual process of maturation, of rereading familiar works in the hope of refining one's taste, deepening one's understanding, and modifying one's judgments, rather than an adventure in intellectual and imaginative exploration.

The non-native reader has corresponding disadvantages and advantages, compared with the native reader. His linguistic and cultural disadvantages are obvious and need to be overcome by effort. However, basically, the difference between reading poetry in one's native language and reading poetry in a foreign language is one of degree rather than kind: even in the former case one still has to make an imaginative leap into a world different from one's own. To a twentieth-century American, Shakespeare's England and Shakespeare's English are less remote than Tang China and classical Chinese, but they still require both consciously obtained knowledge and imaginative effort to be wholly accessible. As for the advantages, the non-native reader is less bound by the Chinese tradition and therefore more free to develop his own tastes and judgments, and he is able to discover new poets and poems for himself, in the same way that I "discovered" Blake for myself. Reading Chinese poetry for a non-native reader can be an exciting experience, which may open up new worlds and new modes of expression. Moreover, since no one uninterested in poetry in his native language is likely to develop an interest in poetry in another language, non-native readers of Chinese poetry may be presumed to be familiar with poetry in English and/or some other language or languages, and should be able to view Chinese poetry in a comparative perspective.

Since in this chapter we are concerned with the critic as reader, we need to consider what reading involves. Some literary theorists and critics, such as Roman Ingarden, Georges Poulet, Wolfgang Iser, and Paul Ricoeur, have dealt with the phenomenology of reading in detail. It is not my intention either to offer an entirely new theory of reading or to repeat or summarize what others have written. I shall simply describe what I think reading, especially reading poetry, entails. As suggested in the previous chapter, reading poetry is not a passive experience of receiving a message or being affected by the work, but an active experience of re-creation. At this point I would like to voice my agreement with those linguists, philosophers of language, and literary theorists who conceive of "meaning" not as an object, not even an intentional object in the phenomenological sense, but as an act. Therefore, instead of asking, "What does this poem mean?" we should rather ask, "What does the author mean by this poem?" To answer this question, we should then ask, "What would I mean by this poem if I were writing it?" This, of course, leads to the question of identification with the author, which we shall consider again in a moment. Meanwhile, let us clarify the interrelations between "world," "meaning," "text," and "poem," with regard to the author in the process of writing, and to the reader in the process of reading.

In the preceding chapter I said that a poem is both referential and self-referential. In its referential aspect, a poem "refers" to a world, by which I do not mean that it merely points to a world, but that it embodies or incarnates a world in its linguistic structure, which, when written down or printed, is the "text." From the author's point of view, "meaning" is an intentional act, which has as its object the poem as a work of art, whereas the text or linguistic structure is only the medium, not the intentional object, as sometimes thought. For the benefit of readers not familiar with phenomenology, it should be pointed out that the terms "intend" and "intentional" as used by phenomenologists do not have their usual meanings in English: to "intend" is to direct one's consciousness toward an object, and the object of such an act is an "intentional object." From the reader's point of view, what he confronts is the text or linguistic structure, which enables him to "re-mean" (at least to some extent) what the author meant, thereby to perceive the "poem" as an aesthetic object, and to re-create the world embodied in the poem.

As Wolfgang Iser has realized, the "poem" (which is both a "work of art" and an "aesthetic object") is the result of an interaction between the "text" and the reader's imagination.[2] This does not mean that there are as many "poems" as there are readers, but that there are as many "concretizations" of the same poem as there are readings (for each reading by the same reader may be different), yet there must be a common core among all the different readings.

So far we have been considering the process of reading poetry with regard to its referential aspect. However, we should not forget its self-referential aspect. In referring to itself, the linguistic structure of a poem enables the reader to satisfy his own creative impulse. This brings us back to the question of identification with the author. I think that the reader identifies with the author in two ways. First, the reader identifies with the author qua speaker of the poem, by "bracketing" (in the Husserlian sense, namely, suspending judgment on) his own lived world and entering the world created by the author. Of course, a reader, being human, cannot totally escape from his own historicity, but it is possible as well as necessary to suspend one's normal beliefs and assumptions and adopt those of the author (or, more strictly speaking, of the speaker). For instance, we need to suspend our belief that the earth is round when reading a poem in which the earth is assumed to be square. It is through the willing suspension of our beliefs (to give Coleridge's phrase a twist) that we can identify with the author qua speaker, for to write is to execute a fiat, and to read is to accept a covenant. The author decrees, "Let there be such-and-such," and the reader has to accept such-and-such as true for the time being, whatever he may believe in normal life. Second, the reader identifies with the author qua author (that is, meaning-giver and creator), by repeating the process of writing, meaning, and creating, as if the reader were now writing, meaning, and creating. It is through this second kind of identification that the reader can share the author's joy of creativity.

Paradoxically, although the reader identifies with the author in the ways suggested above, at the same time he is conscious of the author as an Other speaking. For example, when I am reading Du Fu, I do not literally think that I am Du Fu but only feel as if I were Du Fu speaking, while at the same time I am also conscious of the voice as Du Fu's. Now, if we compare the situation of reading with that of conversation, we seem to encounter a problem. As Husserl observed, in conversation we can only understand the meaning of the word "I" from the living utterance and the circumstances that surround it, and if we read the word without knowing who wrote it, it is perhaps not meaningless but at least estranged from its normal sense.[3] He also pointed out that the conceptual meaning of "I" as "whatever speaker is designating himself" is not the same as what we take the word to mean in an actual utterance.[4] In other words, when we hear the first person pronoun, we take it to mean the person who is speaking, not the abstract concept of "whatever speaker is designating himself." When we turn to Chinese poetry, although the first person pronoun is often omitted, there is still an implied speaker in every poem. Does this mean that we can only understand a poem when we know the identity of the author and the circumstances in which he wrote it? Some scholars who adhere to the historico-biographical approach might answer in the affirmative, but the plain fact that we do understand anonymous poems makes such an answer untenable. To solve this problem we need to recognize three distinctions: first, between the author and the speaker; second, between the specified or intended reader and the implied reader; third, between the actual context in which a poem is written and what we may call the dramatic context in which the speaker is imagined as speaking.

Of course, an author may speak in his own person or adopt a different persona. When he is speaking in his own person, knowledge about his life can affect our understanding of a poem. For instance, the following poem by Li Shangyin (813?–858) may at first sight appear to be a celebration of the simple rustic life:

自喜

自喜蝸牛舍

兼容燕子巢

綠筠遺粉籜

紅藥綻香苞

虎過遙知穽

魚來且佐庖

慢行成酩酊

隣壁有松醪

Zi Xi
Self Joy
zi xi waniu she
self delight snail cottage
jian rong yanzi chao
also allow swallow nest
lü yun yi fen tuo
green bamboo leave powdery skin

hong yao jan xiang bao
red peony burst fragrant bud
hu guo yao zhi jing
tiger pass far know trap
yu lai qie zuo pao
fish come temporarily help kitchen
man xing cheng mingding
slow walk become drunk
lin bi you song lao
next wall have pine wine[5]

Self-congratulation
I congratulate myself on my snail-cottage,
Which also accommodates a swallow's nest.
The green bamboos shed their powdery leaves;
The red peonies burst their fragrant buds.
A tiger passes: aware of the distant trap;
A fish comes: let it enrich my meal.
Walking slowly, I gradually get drunk;
My next door neighbor has a resin wine.[6]

However, when one reads in a letter that Li wrote in 849 to Lu Hong-zhi, military governor of Wuning, who had invited Li to join his staff, that the poet was "being cramped in a rented snail-cottage and living precariously in a swallow's nest," one cannot help suspecting that the title of the poem is ironic: instead of congratulating himself, the poet is really mocking himself and complaining about the straitened circumstances in which he is living. Even if the tone of the poem is not wholly ironic, it is at least ambivalent. On the other hand, the poet seems to enjoy the simple pleasures of a rustic existence and the freedom from political dangers (suggested by the trap); on the other hand, he is far from being content with his living conditions. Without reading the letter, in which the same expressions "snail-cottage" and "swallow's nest" appear as in the poem, we might have missed the irony and the ambivalent attitude of the poet.[7]

Sometimes, even though the author is the speaker, he may simply act as the narrator, such as in Du Fu's famous "Stone-moat Village Officer":

石壕吏

暮投石壕村

有吏夜捉人

老翁踰牆走

老婦出門看

吏呼一何怒

婦啼一何苦

聽婦前致詞

三男鄴城戍

一男附書至

二男新戰死

存者且偷生

死者長已矣

室中更無人

惟有乳下孫

有孫母未去

出入無完裙

老嫗力雖衰

請從吏夜歸

急應河陽役

猶得備晨炊

夜久語聲絕

如聞泣幽咽

天明登前途

獨與老翁別

Shihao li
Stone-moat Officer
mu tou Shihao cun
evening rush Stone-moat village
you li ye zhuo ren
there-is officer night catch men
lao weng yu qiang zou

old man climb wall flee
lao fu chu men kan
old woman go-out door look
li hu yihe nu
officer shout how angry
fu ti yihe ku
woman cry how bitter
ting fu qian zhi ci
listen woman forward address speech
san nan Ye cheng shu
three son Ye city guard
yi nan fu shu zhi
one son attach letter come
er nan xin zhan si
two son newly battle die
cunzhe qie tou sheng
survivor temporarily steal life
sizhe chang yiyi
dead-ones long finish-over
shi zhong geng wu ren
room inside again no person
wei you ruxia sun
only have milk-under grandson
sun you mu wei qu
grandson have mother not-yet leave
chu ru wu wan qun
go-out come-in no whole skirt
lao yu li sui shuai
old woman though strength weak
qing cong li ye gui
beg follow officer night return
ji ying Heyang yi
hasten answer Heyang service
you de bei chen chui
yet able prepare morning cook
ye jiu yu sheng jue
night long talk sound stop
ru wen qi yuye
seem hear weep choke-sob
tianming deng qian tu

dawn go-on front way
du yu lao weng bie
alone with old man part[8]

At nightfall, I rushed toward Stone-moat Village;
There was an officer catching men at night.
An old man climbed over the wall and fled;
An old woman came out of the door to look.
The officer's yell: how angry!
The woman's cry: how bitter!
"Listen to me as I come forth to speak:
My three sons went to guard the town of Ye.
One son had a letter brought by a friend:
The other two had recently died in battle.
We the living live on stolen time,
They the dead are finished forever.
There is no man left in the house,
Only my grandson, a mere suckling.
His mother has not gone away,
She goes about without an untorn skirt.
Although I, an old woman, am weak,
I'm willing to go back with you by night,
To answer the urgent call from Heyang:
I'll be in time to cook breakfast tomorrow."
As night wore on, sound of talk ceased:
I seemed to hear choking sobs.
At dawn I went on my way,
And said goodbye to the old man alone.[9]

It is not necessary to know anything about Du Fu's own life in order
to understand this poem, since he is acting as the narrator and serving
as a bridge between the world of the poem and the world of the reader. Having introduced us to the world of the poem, the poet withdraws
and lets the old woman take over the role of the speaker, so that we
can learn her pathetic story from her own lips. At the end of the poem,
the poet reappears to lead us out of the world of the poem again. The
poet's sympathy for the old woman and her family is implicit in the
poem, and we need no extraneous knowledge about Du Fu's attitude
toward war.

When a poet assumes a dramatic persona, such as in the following poem by Li Bo (701–762), it is not necessary to know about his own life:

長安一片月
萬戶擣衣聲
秋風吹不盡
總是玉關情
何日平胡虜
良人罷遠征

Chang'an yi pian yue
Chang'an one swath moon
wan hu dao yi sheng
myriad door pound clothes sound
qiu feng chui bu jin
autumn wind blow not exhaust
zong shi Yuguan qing
generally is Yuguan feeling
he ri ping hu lu
what day suppress barbarian slave
liangren ba yuan zheng
husband stop far campaign[10]

Chang'an in a swath of moonlight;
From ten thousand houses, the sound of pounding clothes.
What the autumn wind cannot fully blow away
Are all feelings about the Jade Pass.
When will the barbarians be suppressed?
No more distant campaigns for my husband then.

All that the reader needs to know is that the speaker is a woman in the imperial capital Chang'an, thinking of her husband far away guarding the frontier, represented by the Jade Pass (Yuguan). Li Bo's own biography is irrelevant to our understanding of this poem.

   Indeed, it is not always necessary even to identify the sex of the speaker of a poem, such as this anonymous poem from the *Book of Poetry* (*Shijing*, ca. 1100–600 B.C.):

野有蔓草
零露漙兮
有美一人
清揚婉兮
邂逅相遇
適我願兮

野有蔓草
零露瀼瀼
有美一人
婉如清揚
邂逅相遇
與子偕臧

ye you man cao
wild there-is creeping grass
ling lu tuan xi
drop dew round ah
you mei yi ren
there-is beauty one person
qingyang wan xi
bright-eyed beautiful ah
xiegou xiang yu
by-chance mutually meet
shi wo yuan xi
suit my wish ah

ye you man cao
wild there-is creeping grass
ling lu rangrang
drop dew plenty
you mei yi ren
there-is beauty one person
wanru qingyang
beautifully bright-eyed
xiegou xiang yu
by-chance mutually meet
yu zi xie zang
with you together hide[11]

In the wilds is a creeper—
The fallen dews are round.
There is one so lovely,
Bright-eyed and beautiful.
By chance we met each other,
And my wish was fulfilled.

In the wilds is a creeper—
The fallen dews are plenty.
There is one so lovely,
Beautiful and bright-eyed.
By chance we met each other,
Let me hide away with you![12]

The original gives no clear indications whether the speaker is a man or a woman, but this does not affect the way in which the poem successfully conveys the lover's joy and desire to be with the loved one. The lack of specific details is but one example of what Roman Ingarden called "spots of indeterminacy,"[13] which are found in all literary works of art and which each reader can fill in according to his imagination.

The question whether a poet is speaking in his own person or assuming a dramatic persona is not always easy to answer. When there are explicit references to persons, events, and places that can be corroborated from other sources, we may assume that the author is speaking in his own person. Nonetheless, some allowance must be made for poetic license, and it would be unwise to identify the created world of the poem with the lived world of the poet. In contrast, when the speaker of a poem is a woman but the author is known to be a man, it is obvious that he is assuming a dramatic persona. Whether he is doing so for allegorical purposes or not must be judged on an individual basis, and the only generalization that can be made is that when a poet assumes a dramatic persona, it is not necessarily for an allegorical purpose but may be simply to dramatize the situation and present it in a more effective way.

Turning to the distinction between the specified reader and the implied reader, we should realize that countless Chinese poems are addressed to individuals, who may be called specified readers. On the other hand, just as every speech act implies a hearer, so does every poem imply a reader, even if it is the author himself, who cannot help being his own first reader. When someone reads a poem, he becomes the actualization of the implied reader. Two questions may be raised here. First, does the actual reader identify with the specified reader? Second, does the actual reader need to know anything about the specified reader? I am not sure about the answer to the first question. I myself always identify with the speaker of the poem, even when I know the author to be a woman. But one woman student told me that when she read Shakespeare's sonnets as a young girl she imagined them to be addressed to her. In other words she identified with the specified reader rather than with the speaker. Perhaps individuals differ in this regard. As for the second question, I think it is sometimes, though not always, necessary to know who the specified reader was and what his relationship with the author was. For instance, in one of a pair of poems entitled "Dreaming of Li Bo," Du Fu wrote,

千秋萬歲名
寂寞身後事

qian qiu wan sui ming
thousand autumn myriad year fame
jimo shen hou shi
quiet life after thing[14]

Fame that lasts a thousand, a myriad years
Is what comes after a life of obscurity.[15]

If we did not know that these two men are generally considered the two greatest poets of China and that neither was successful in his official career, the lines would lose much of their poignancy and tragic irony, created by Du Fu's awareness of his own and Li Bo's greatness and his disappointment at the failures of both their lives.

As for the distinction between the actual context and the dramatic context of a poem, the former refers to the actual circumstances in which a poem was written, the latter to the dramatic situation in which the speaker is imagined as speaking. Chinese poets often do inform us, in the title or a note or a preface, of the actual context in which a poem was written. Such information can be very helpful to our understanding of a poem. For example, in a preface to a group of poems entitled "Willow Branch," Li Shangyin tells us how he met a girl named Willow Branch (Liuzhi), who admired his poetry, how he missed a rendezvous with her, and how she became a nobleman's concubine.[16] Without this preface we would not have known that the title refers to a woman's name, nor would we have understood the specific implications of some of the images used. Sometimes a preface can throw light on a poet's creative process. The poet, composer, and critic Jiang Kui is particularly fond of attaching prefaces to his lyrics (*ci*). As Shuen-fu Lin has demonstrated in his book on Jiang, some of the prefaces can be considered artistic entities in themselves, and others only provide external references.[17] The latter kind can inform us how the poet-composer proceeded: whether he first composed the music and then set it to words, or wrote words to fit existing music, as most Chinese lyricists did.

Of course, it is not always possible to know the actual context in which a poem was written, but it is not always necessary to know either. Often the poem itself provides sufficient indications of the dramatic context in which the speaker is imagined as speaking, such as in this poem by Cui Hao (ob. 754):

君家在何處
妾住在橫塘
停船暫借問
或恐是同鄉

jun jia he chu zhu
your home what place live
qie zhu zai Hengtang
I live at Level-dike
ting chuan zhan jie wen
stop boat momentarily borrow ask
huo kong shi tong xiang
perhaps fear be same village[18]

Where, sir, is your home?
I live by the Level-Dike.
Let me stop my boat and ask you for a moment:
Perhaps we both come from the same town?

In the original, the speaker is clearly indicated to be a woman by the word *qie*, which means literally "handmaid" or "concubine" but was used conventionally as a way for a woman to refer to herself, tantamount to a first person pronoun. Once we realize that the speaker is a woman, it is easy to see the dramatic context in which she is speaking: she is addressing some man to whom she has obviously taken a fancy, and is using the question about where his home is as an excuse to make his acquaintance. When reading poems like this, there is no need to know what the actual context of the poem was.

In short, how much we need to know about the author, the specified reader, and the actual context of a poem depends on the nature of the poem itself. Although we may use biographical data to help us understand a poem, we should guard against the danger of falling into the vicious circle of deducing biographical data from the poet's works and then reading his works in the light of the supposed biography. Further, it should be realized that knowing about an author's life as a person is not the same as being able to recognize his voice as a poet. The latter means being familiar with his linguistic habits, such as his favorite expressions, his use of imagery, his handling of syntax and of allusions, and, most elusive of all, his typical tone. Just as in everyday conversation the more one knows about a speaker's speech habits, the better one will understand what he says, so in reading poetry the more one knows about the author's linguistic habits, the better one will understand what he writes. Only long immersion in a poet's works can give one such knowledge.

This may be the appropriate time to raise another question: is it necessary to know the traditional genre to which a Chinese poem supposedly belongs, in order to arrive at what E. D. Hirsch, Jr., calls the "intrinsic genre"?[19] Before attempting to answer this question, we need to clarify what is meant by "genre." Critics writing in English about Chinese poetry are far from being unanimous in their use of the term. Sometimes, different verse forms, such as *guti shi* (Ancient Style Verse) and *jinti shi* (Recent Style Verse) are referred to as "genres," but at other times poems on different subjects, such as *huaigu shi* ("poems recalling antiquity") and *yongwu shi* ("poems singing of objects") are called "genres." When we turn to traditional Chinese criticism, there is no clear and consistent definition of "genre" either. The word that corresponds to "genre" is *ti*, which, however, is sometimes closer to "style" in English. It may refer to the style of a period, such as *Jian'an ti* (the Jian'an style), or the style of an individual poet, such as *Taibo ti* (Li Bo's style), or that of a school, such as *Xikun ti* (the style of the Xikun School, who imitated Li Shangyin), or that of poetry on a particular subject, such as *xianglian ti* (the style of boudoir verse). In anthologies and editions of the collected works of poets, poems may be classified on the basis of form, or subject, or chronology. Similarly, literary theorists who drew up lists of genres did not follow a single criterion but used formal, thematic, or historical criteria as they wished.[20] Modern Chinese literary historians and critics, influenced by the nineteenth-century European evolutionary view of literature, have attempted to trace the origin and evolution of each literary genre as if it were a biological species. Actually, literary genres are neither biological species nor a priori categories, but convenient labels applied post hoc to existing bodies of works. Hence, any attempt to define precisely the exact nature of a genre or the Platonic Idea behind it is foredoomed to failure. However, we need not go to the opposite extreme, as did Croce, who thought genres no more meaningful than the arrangement of books in a library.[21] Diachronically, "genres" represent what poets and critics of given periods perceived to be the appropriate interrelations between forms, subjects, and styles. These interrelations may change when an innovative poet appears. For instance, the *ci* or "lyric" was at first considered suitable only for the expression of romantic love, but Su Shi (1037–1101) showed that it was possible to write on historical and philosophical themes in lyric meters.[22] Synchronically, if we adopt the concept of poetry as the overlapping of linguistic structure and artistic function, then "genres" may be conceived of as the overlapping of specific linguistic structures and specific artistic functions. Faced with a traditional Chinese generic term, no matter whether it primarily denotes a form, a subject, or a style, we can ask what its distinctive linguistic features, thematic range, stylistic traits, and artistic effects are. This will guide us in our expectations of a given poem and help us arrive at the "intrinsic genre." Thus, we have answered, at least partially, the question posed earlier. However, our expectations based on knowledge of traditional genres may be frustrated, for a poet may surprise us by breaking conventions and establishing new interrelations between form, subject, and style. Traditional generic labels are only rough guides, not infallible ones.

Furthermore, since poetic genres do not come into being or cease to exist at precise moments in history, generic distinctions cannot be clear-cut, and some borderline cases are bound to appear. In such cases, the correct assignment of a particular poem to a particular genre is a matter of interest to literary historians rather than critics, for our understanding of a poem need not be greatly affected by knowledge of the genre to which it is supposed to belong. For example, the following poem, entitled "Grievance on the Marble Steps" (*Yujie yuan*), by Xie Tiao (464–499) is considered a "Music Department" song (*yuefu*):[23]

夕殿下珠簾
流螢飛復息
長夜縫羅衣
思君此何極

xi dian xia zhu lian
evening palace lower pearl curtain
liu ying fei fu xi
drifting glowworm fly again stop
chang ye feng luo yi
long night sew silk clothes
si jun ci he ji
think you this how end[24]

In the evening palace, I lower the pearl curtain.
Drifting glowworms fly, then cease.
All night long I sew the silk gown,
Think of you—how can this end?

Yet it is practically indistinguishable from a Quatrain (*jueju*), a subdivision of Recent Style Verse, so much so that the critic Shen Deqian (1673–1769) commented: "This is virtually a Tang Quatrain; among Tang poets this would be considered of the highest quality."[25] The only reason why Xie Tiao's poem is not called a Quatrain is that in his time the Recent Style Verse had not yet been fully established as a major verse form. If a reader ignorant of this fact of literary history mistook the poem for a Quatrain, his understanding of it would not be seriously affected. Likewise, Li Bo's poem bearing the same title is sometimes classified both as a *yuefu* and a *jueju*,[26] but one's understanding of it would not be different whether one thought it was the former or the latter:

玉階生白露
夜久侵羅襪
卻下水晶簾
玲瓏望秋月

yu jie sheng bai lu
marble step grow white dew
ye jiu qin luo wa
night long invade silk stocking
que xia shuijing lian
still lower crystal curtain
linglong wang qiu yue
glitter gaze autumn moon[27]

On marble steps white dew grows.
Deep in the night, it soaks silk stockings.
Yet she lowers the crystal curtain—
Glittering—to gaze at the autumn moon.

Both poems embody a similar world and both share certain formal features, so that the identification of the genre to which each belongs does not much affect our understanding of either. But when it comes to evaluating each poem in terms of its importance in literary history, it will then be relevant to ask how far each poet has contributed to the development of the genre as a whole.

3

The Critic as Translator

MUCH HAS BEEN written about translation in general and the translation of Chinese poetry into English in particular. I do not intend to revive all the old controversies about how to translate Chinese poetry, or to repeat everything that I have written on the subject, but to try to clarify a few basic issues concerning the translation of Chinese poetry by discussing them within the conceptual framework of this book. However, in order to make the discussion intelligible to readers not familiar with my previous writings, it will be necessary for me to reiterate certain points that I have made before.

I should like to begin by drawing a distinction between the poet as translator (or poet-translator for short) and the critic as translator (critic-translator) and pointing out that they have different aims and different readerships.[1] The poet-translator is a poet or poet manqué whose native Muse is temporarily or permanently absent and who uses translation as a way to recharge his own creative battery. His primary aim is to write a good poem in English based on his understanding or misunderstanding of a Chinese poem, however he may have arrived at this. A critic-translator is a critic writing in English about Chinese poetry. His primary aim is to show what the original poem is like, as a part of his interpretation. As for their respective readers, the poet-translator aims at those who cannot read Chinese but enjoy reading poetry in English, whereas the critic-translator may have several kinds of readers: English-speaking students of Chinese poetry

37

struggling with the original texts and needing guidance and help, specialists who wish to compare someone else's interpretations and evaluations of Chinese poetry with their own, and those who cannot read Chinese but are seriously interested in learning more about it for comparative or other scholarly purposes rather than simple enjoyment. The first kind of readers, including most book reviewers for the popular press and for journals not devoted to Asian studies, are in no position to know, and perhaps do not care, how far a translation resembles the original, and when they say a work is a good translation, what they really mean is that it reads well in English. The other kinds of readers need to know how far a translation resembles the original and not simply how well it reads in English.

The two kinds of translators are, of course, not mutually exclusive. Ideally, they should coincide: the same translator should be a competent critic of Chinese poetry and a competent poet in English, but in actual fact there has rarely been a translator who translated directly from the Chinese unaided and who is also an established poet in English in his own right. Gary Snyder seems to be the only exception, but even his translations are not free from errors that are obviously due to misunderstandings of the original texts and not to poetic license. Other translators of Chinese poetry form a whole spectrum, from the freely inventing Pound at one extreme to the uncompromisingly prosaic Karlgren at the other. On the whole, poet-translators, who may know some Chinese or none at all, such as Pound, Amy Lowell, Witter Bynner, and Kenneth Rexroth, have either reworked existing translations by scholars or had collaborators. Unfortunately, the collaborators or "native informants" they chose have not always turned out to be well-informed about Chinese poetry. Then there are some translators who appear to aim primarily at producing poetic English versions of Chinese poetry, such as Arthur Waley, David Hawkes, A. C. Graham, Burton Watson, and Jonathan Chaves, yet none of them is well known as a poet in his own right. Apart from a few early poems that he wrote as an undergraduate at Cambridge and one or two self-parodies, Waley did not publish his own poetry; Graham has published at least one original poem; the others, as far as I know, have not published original poetry. Turning to critic-translators, such as Hans Frankel and Stephen Owen, they naturally also wish to produce readable English versions of Chinese poetry, but their primary concern is to demonstrate certain features and qualities of the original poems, rather than writing good poems in English. It is, of course, with the last kind of translator that I identify myself.

Since the poet-translator and the critic-translator have different aims and different readerships, they naturally differ in the ways they translate. Two examples should suffice to illustrate this point. First, when faced with a cliché in Chinese, a poet-translator would probably try to improve it and not replace it with an English cliché, whereas a critic-translator would hesitate to improve the original but feel obliged to point out that it is a cliché. Second, in the case of allusions, with which Chinese poetry is replete, a poet-translator would avoid cumbersome footnotes but either paraphrase or incorporate whatever explanation he thinks necessary in the translation itself, whereas a critic-translator would preserve all the allusions and then add notes or commentaries to explain their significance and poetic functions.

Perhaps we can now lay to rest the ancient dispute between "literal" and "free" translations, or at least discuss the question in different terms. Rather than asking whether a translation should be "literal" or "free," we should ask what linguistic structures fulfil what poetic functions in the original, and what linguistic structures in English can fulfil similar poetic functions. A poet-translator would probably not be overconcerned with the first question but would address himself to the second question, using any linguistic structures in English that he thought could best fulfil the desired poetic functions. By contrast, a critic-translator would consider it his duty to show how certain poetic functions are fulfilled by certain linguistic structures in the original, whether such structures can be reproduced in English or not, and whether, if reproduced, they can fulfil similar poetic functions in English or not. He may have to choose between two alternatives: either to reproduce the original linguistic structures, if possible, no matter whether they are poetically effective in English or not, while informing the reader how they work in the original, or to substitute different linguistic structures in English, which he hopes will fulfil similar poetic functions, and then inform the reader that these functions are fulfilled by other linguistic means in the original.

It should be obvious from the above discussions that the interrelations between linguistic structures and poetic functions are complex and changeable, and that it is a fallacy to think that by reproducing the original linguistic structures of poetry one will automatically re-produce the original poetic effects. Such a fallacy seems to underlie the tendency that I have termed "barbarization," by which I mean the attempt to reshape the English language so as to preserve the linguis-tic structures of Chinese poetry and its underlying ways of thinking and feeling. The opposite tendency, which I have called "naturaliza-tion" refers to the attempt to turn Chinese poetry into English poetry without violating existing conventions of the English language.[2] For those who advocate naturalization, "the first requisite of a translation is that it should not sound like a translation," as Marianne Moore put it,[3] but to those who favor barbarization, a translation *should* sound like a translation and not an original English poem. Let us widen the scope of our discussion for a moment and consider briefly translations from and into other languages. Historically, most success-ful English translators of poetry from other languages, from Chapman through Dryden and Pope to FitzGerald, were naturalizers, although barbarization was not absent, a notable example being the King James Version of the Bible. On the theoretical level, barbarization found an advocate in Robert Browning, if the account given by John Adding-ton Symonds is accurate: "Browning's theory of translation. Ought to be absolutely literal, with exact renderings of words, and words placed in the order of the original. Only a rendering of this sort gives any real insight into the original."[4] This, of course, assumes that one can draw exact equations between words of one language and those of another, and that the same word order in one language will mean the same thing in another. If only this were true! In the twentieth cen-tury, Walter Benjamin quoted with approval Rudolph Pannwitz's observation that German translators should not try to turn Hindi, Greek, or English into German but do the reverse, so as to expand and deepen the native language by means of the foreign one.[5]

To turn back to translations of Chinese poetry: the earlier transla-tors, such as James Legge and H. A. Giles, put their translations into traditional English meters and adopted pseudoarchaic diction, so that their translations now generally read like parodies of polite Victorian verse. More recent translators, from Arthur Waley to present-day trans-lators (with a few exceptions like Alan Ayling and Duncan Mack-intosh), have eschewed traditional English meters and rhymes but adopted sprung rhythm verse or experimented with other kinds of modern English verse. However, most of them share a common aim: to write English poetry. No one can object to such a laudable aim, but the question is, how far should one go in naturalizing Chinese poetry, with its different linguistic structure, different modes of thinking and feeling, and different ways of expression? Should one turn unfamiliar concepts and attitudes, exotic imagery, recondite allusions, and ambiguous syntax into familiar and easily comprehensible ones? Surely it is going too far to translate *shunü* ("virtuous girl") as "Nymph" and *junzi* ("lord's son" or "young lord") as "Shepherd," as one recent translator did,[6] so that a Greco-Roman world is substituted for the ancient Chinese one? By the same token, should one not also substitute "rose" for "lotus," "golden tresses" for "cloudy hair," and "Diana" for "Chang'e"? Is it too much to expect readers of translations of Chinese poetry to learn the symbolic values and emotional associations of images and the significance of allusions? If all that such readers want is English poetry of a familiar and conventional kind, why should they bother to read translations of Chinese poetry at all?

As far as verse form is concerned, David Hawkes has put the case for naturalization well:

> Of course, no translation from the Chinese, whatever the genre, can be formally *like* the original. Five-stressed verses in sprung rhythm are no more *like* Chinese pentasyllabics than iambic pentameters or stanzas in common metre. A translator can only choose or invent a form in which he can best express to his own satisfaction the "feeling" that he is given by the original. The measure of his success has very little to do with the number of formal elements that the original and the translation have in common.[7]

Granted that the "feeling" one gets from any verse form in English can never be demonstrably "like" that which one gets from a Chinese verse form, it still seems to me that the translation should bear some formal resemblance to the original. For instance, to turn a compact antithetical couplet from a Chinese poem in Regulated Verse into several loosely constructed lines of free verse is to change the character of the verse completely, but to turn it into two compact and paratactic lines of English verse would preserve at least some of the original "feeling."

Not all poet-translators and those who aspire to be such are naturalizers; some of them, from the Imagists to the "Syntaxists" (those who believe that translations of Chinese poetry should follow the original syntax), are barbarizers, in practice or in theory, if not both. There are two main arguments for barbarization: first, that it will revitalize the English language and initiate a new kind of poetry and a new poetics; second, that it is only by barbarization that one can preserve the true nature of Chinese poetry. Since we are concerned here with the interpretation of Chinese poetry and not with its effect on modern American or British poetry, we need not consider the first argument but have to consider the second.

I have no wish to deny that, as Wai-lim Yip and others have asserted, Chinese poetry enjoys a high degree of syntactic fluidity, or that a translator can unwittingly impose a Western mode of thought and perception on Chinese poetry by introducing such grammatical features as tense, number, conjunctions, articles, and pronouns, which are absent in the original.[8] After all, it was I who first suggested that the absence of tense, number, subject, and so on gave some Chinese poetry an impersonal, timeless, and universal character.[9] However, I think we should not exaggerate this aspect of Chinese poetry, or rather, we should not pay attention exclusively to this kind of Chinese poetry. There are intensely personal, as well as narrative and even discursive, poems in Chinese. Similarly, we should not exaggerate the intuitive and nonrational character of Chinese thought: one cannot ignore the long tradition of Confucian rationalism, which found expression in some poems. Furthermore, even the most intuitive kind of poetry, which gives the *impression* of being impersonal, timeless, and universal, cannot literally present what Yip calls "pure experience" or "pure Phenomenon" unmediated by language, because language *is* mediation between the speaker and the world. A poet may wish to create the illusion that the reader is in direct contact with experience or phenomenon, but actually no one can write poetry without some degree of conceptualization. On the practical level, we may formulate the question thus: is it either absolutely necessary or always possible to follow Chinese syntax in translations of Chinese poetry, so as to preserve its underlying mode of perception?

The answer to the first part of the question is that it depends on what semantic and poetic functions the original syntax fulfils. Sometimes it is necessary to keep the original syntax, such as in the line

青青河畔草

qing qing he pan cao
green green river side grass[10]

which first presents a sense impression, then locates it, and finally
identifies the object that causes it, so that the reader feels as if he were
experiencing the scene directly. The effect of the original can be
largely preserved if we translate it as

Green, green: the riverside grass,

where the only concession to English grammar and idiom, the addi-
tion of the definite article, does not alter or detract from the original
effect. But if we translate the line as

The grass by the river is very green,

then it becomes an assertion, and the reader will feel that he is being
told something instead of experiencing it. In other cases, however, the
semantic and poetic functions of a line can be preserved, or even better served, by syntactic changes in the translation. The last line of
Du Fu's "Stone-moat Village Officer," which was quoted in the preceding chapter, reads in the original:

du yu lao weng bie
alone with old man part

If we should translate this as

Alone with the old man I parted

it would not bring out the point that the speaker said goodbye to the
old man alone because the old woman had left, apart from being un-
idiomatic. That is why I translated it as

And said goodbye to the old man alone.

Irving Lo's version, "Only the old man was there to see me off,"[11] can
be justified on similar grounds.

Indeed, it can be positively misleading at times to follow the original syntax and word order. For example, the phrase *shan shang ren* means "man on mountain": to follow the original word order and translate it as "mountain on man" would turn it into nonsense.

If a critic-translator provides the reader with the original text, transliterations, and word-for-word versions, as various recent translators, including myself, have done, then even those who cannot read Chinese will be able to see what the original syntax is, and some concessions to English grammar and idiom can be made in a more "readable" version.

As for whether it is always possible to reproduce Chinese syntax, the answer is no, for sometimes a line in Chinese can be syntactically construed in several ways simultaneously, and no translation can preserve such syntactic ambiguity. A famous example is Wang Wei's

日色冷青松

ri se leng qing song
sun color chill green pine[12]

which can be construed as "sun's color chills green pines," or "sun's color chills among green pines," or "sun's color is chilled by green pines." The poet is not concerned with the question which object is chilled by which, but with presenting a single experience that fuses the impressions of pale sunlight, chilliness, and green pines. In the original, the word *leng* ("chill") has a pivotal role, pointing both forward to *qing song* ("green pines") and backward to *ri se* ("sun's color").[13] It is simply impossible to do this in English: one has to decide whether "chill" is a transitive verb or an intransitive one, whether it is active voice or passive voice, whether it is a verb or an adjective, and whether the line is a sentence or two noun phrases. In such cases, the critic-translator can only describe what he cannot reproduce.

Earlier on I referred to the absence of tense and number in Chinese poetry; one or two points in this connection should be clarified. By the "absence of tense" I meant, of course, the absence of tense inflections in classical Chinese verbs, not the absence of any awareness of temporal relations between what is spoken of and the time of speaking. If we accept the definition of tense given recently by a linguist as "the semantactic category that establishes the relationship which holds between the situation or event talked about and the time of utterance,"[14] then we obviously have to admit that tense is present in at least some Chinese poems, with the proviso that "time of utterance" must be understood in a double sense: from the author's point of view, it refers to the historical moment when the poem was written, but from the reader's point of view, it refers to the time of reading, when the reader, identifying with the speaker of the poem or at least imagining the speaker as speaking, revives the moment of writing. Thus, when reading a poem, we have to take any temporal deictic term there may be as if it referred to *our* present rather than the author's. For example, the expression *jinri* ("today") has to be taken as if it referred to our "today," even if the author or some conscientious commentator tells us the exact date when the poem was written. The historical date of writing can, of course, be relevant to the interpretation of the poem, but at the moment of reading we have to temporarily forget that the poem was written so many years ago, but feel as if that date were now. It is a paradox that although all poetry is timeless in one sense, as I suggested in the introduction, in another sense poetry explores different ways of perceiving time. In fact, an enquiry into the way or ways in which a poet orients himself to time in a given poem provides one of the most helpful means of entry into the world of that poem, as we shall see in the final chapter.

As for the "absence of number," this refers not to the absence of numerals but to the fact that Chinese nouns do not have singular and plural forms. It is, of course, perfectly possible to indicate number if desired. For instance, in the Quatrain "Sitting Alone at Jingting Mountain," Li Bo uses several words to specify number:

衆鳥高飛盡
孤雲獨去閒
相看兩不厭
只有敬亭山

zhong niao gao fei jin
many bird high fly finish
gu yun du qu xian
solitary cloud alone depart at-ease
xiang kan liang bu yan
mutually watch both not tired

zhi you Jingting shan
only there-is Jingting mountain[15]

Flocks of birds, flying high, are all gone.
A single cloud alone departs at ease.
Watching each other, neither getting tired:
Only the Jingting Mountain and I.

The contrast between *zhong* ("many, multitudinous, crowd, flock")
and *gu* ("solitary") emphasizes the contrast between the multitude of
birds and the solitude of the cloud. This probably symbolizes the contrast between the common crowd of people and the solitary speaker
himself. The solitude of the cloud (speaker) is further emphasized by
the word *du* ("alone"). This sense of solitude is attenuated by the
feeling of communion with the mountain, which is brought out by the
words *xiang* ("mutually") and *liang* ("two, both"). Yet some feeling
of isolation remains, as suggested by the word *zhi* ("only"): the speaker and the mountain may have each other for company but they are
cut off from everyone else.

Sometimes one can tell the number of a noun from the context or
from conventional associations. For example, any experienced reader
seeing the word *yuanyang* ("mandarin duck") would assume it to be
dual, since the male and female of this species conventionally sym-
bolize husband and wife or a pair of lovers. More often, Chinese poets
leave number unspecified because it is poetically irrelevant. Despite
the objection that Burton Watson raised some time ago,[16] I still think
that in Wang Wei's lines

月出驚山鳥
時鳴春澗中

yue chu jing shan niao
moon rise surprise mountain bird
shi ming chun jian zhong
occasionally cry spring valley inside[17]

Moon rise surprise (s) mountain bird (s),
Occasionally cry in spring valley

it is of no consequence whether we take *niao* ("bird") as singular or
plural.[18] In any case, I do not believe that poetic imagery has to be

visualized in order to be effective. How are we supposed to visualize the following?

> I have no spur
> To prick the sides of my intent, but only
> Vaulting ambition, which o'erleaps itself
> And falls on the other. . . .[19]

And even when number is specified, we need not visualize the image. When Romeo says of Juliet's eyes:

> Two of the fairest stars in all the heaven
> Having some business, do entreat her eyes
> To twinkle in their spheres till they return,[20]

are we supposed to visualize two big eyes twinkling in the sky? In Chinese poetry, the effect of imagery often depends on symbolic significance and emotional associations rather than visual appeal. Besides, as Roman Ingarden pointed out, it is in lyric poetry that "spots of indeterminacy," which need to be filled in by the reader's imagination, are of the greatest importance.[21]

What has been said above about syntax also applies to other aspects of the linguistic structure of a poem, such as prosodic features. Some prosodic features of Chinese verse, notably tonal patterns, simply cannot be reproduced in English. Other features like alliteration and rhyme can be reproduced, but it is questionable whether they have the same effect in English as in Chinese. End-rhyme, which is ubiquitous in classical Chinese poetry except for a few very early poems, can be reproduced in English, but this is often achieved at the cost of distortion of meaning, unnatural inversions, omissions, or padding. What is more, English rhymes, especially masculine rhymes in couplets, tend to have a jingling and comic effect, which is not the case with Chinese rhymes. That is why so many rhymed translations of Chinese poetry sound like doggerel. (It is, of course, an entirely different matter when a translator of Chinese fiction or drama deliberately uses doggerel to indicate the poor quality of the original.) This does not mean that translations of Chinese poetry should never use rhyme, but only that one should consider what effect the original rhymes produce, and experiment with rhyme as well as other devices like slanting rhyme and assonance to achieve a similar effect. But however successful he may be in this respect, a critic-translator would still feel obliged to describe the prosodic features of the original poem and their poetic effects.

Whereas translators of Chinese poetry have always paid great attention to imagery and, more recently, to syntax, few have paid sufficient attention to two other aspects of poetic language: the level of diction and the poet's general tone in a poem.[22] Chinese poets did not employ a uniformly "poetic" diction, but varied from the archaic to the colloquial. Even the same poet may use different levels of diction according to the theme and genre of the poem. True enough, as Burton Watson has observed, that it is difficult to know how far apart the literary and spoken languages may have been at any given period, but we do have some notion as to the degree of formality or colloquialism of the language of a poem. When Cao Cao (155–220) wrote in the meter of the *Book of Poetry* and incorporated lines from it verbatim in his own poetry, we can be quite sure that he was not writing in the colloquial language of his time. I am not suggesting that classical Chinese should be rendered into Anglo-Saxon or pseudoarchaic English, but only that translations should reflect to some extent the degree of formality or colloquialism, elegance or plainness, sophistication or simplicity, of the original. Presumably, contemporary English is capable of such distinctions, and not all contemporary American and British poets write in a uniformly colloquial style. Hence, to be noncolloquial is not necessarily the same as being noncontemporary, as some recent translators appear to think. Such translators would condemn any translation that does not use a strictly contemporary colloquial idiom as pedantic or pompous, without asking whether the original is formal, or colloquial, or consciously archaistic. Similarly, a translator should consider the tone of the poem: whether it is solemn, or lighthearted, or intimate, or ironic, and so on. The translation should adopt a similar tone and not aim at a "poetic" tone of its own. One should not forget that it is the interactions among various linguistic elements that produce the total effect of a poem, and although these elements are not all equally translatable, some consideration should be given each.

In brief, the critic-translator stands in the same relation to his reader as the original author stands in relation to the critic-as-reader.

The critic-translator's task is to bridge the gulf between the world of the poem and the world of the reader, and to describe, if he cannot reproduce, the original linguistic structure that embodies the poetic world. Since the kinds of readers for whom the critic-translator writes are presumably seeking knowledge and not just pleasure, it is more important for the critic-translator to instruct than to please. To him, translation is not an end in itself but part of the interpretative process. Finally, it may be added that there can never be a definitive translation of any poem, just as there can never be a definitive interpretation of any poem. However, this does not mean that all versions and perversions are equally acceptable, any more than that all interpretations and misinterpretations are equally valid.

4

The Critic as Interpreter

THE IMPORTANCE of interlingual interpretation can hardly be exaggerated. A moment's reflection will make one realize that some, if not most, of the world's most influential books, such as the Bible, Buddhist sutras, the Confucian Canon, and the works of Marx, Lenin, Freud, and Mao, have been known to innumerable readers only through translations and interlingual interpretations. With regard to purely literary works, all modern studies of classical and medieval European literature are written in languages other than those in which the works studied were written. And how many English-speaking readers are able to read Homer, Dante, Goethe, Tolstoy, Ibsen, and Camus, to mention but a few, all in the original languages? Yet these authors undoubtedly form part of the literary consciousness and experience of every literate reader whose native language is English. In recent years, many readers have also become aware of, if not familiar with, such masterpieces of Asian literature as *The Tale of Genji* and *Dream of the Red Chamber* (more accurately, *A Red Mansion Dream,* also known as *The Story of the Stone*). As far as Chinese poetry is concerned, it is too optimistic to hope that the majority of English-speaking readers will ever learn to read Chinese; therefore, interpretations in English of Chinese poetry will continue to be needed. Indeed, demands for such interpretations will increase if interest in things Chinese continues to grow. Now, interpretation is, of course, a critic's main task. Some would even say that it is his only task, but, as I have indicated before, interpretation necessarily entails evaluation, and a critic has to undertake both tasks. However, in the present chapter we shall concern ourselves only with some problems of interpretation that a critic writing in English about Chinese poetry has to face.

The problems of interpretation facing an intralingual critic are formidable enough; they become doubly so for the interlingual critic, since to the problems due to differences between historical periods are added those due to cultural and linguistic differences. The interlingual critic has to make a decision as to what basic attitude he should take toward such differences, and the decision will determine the kind of interpretation that he will offer. It is not an easy decision to make, for even within a single cultural and literary tradition there can be conflicting schools of hermeneutics. In the Western tradition, as Peter Szondi demonstrated, there was a conflict between the historico-philological and the allegorical schools of hermeneutics.[1] In China, a similar conflict existed during the Qing (Ch'ing) period (1644–1911) between the so-called Han and Song (Sung) schools of Confucian scholarship, the former emphasizing philology and textual criticism, the latter philosophical and often allegorical interpretation. In recent times, various schools of criticism, such as the Freudian and the archetypal, can be considered modern variations of the allegorical school. Marxist criticism presents something of a paradox: to the extent that Marxist critics interpret literary works by referring to the socioeconomic and political environments in which these were produced, their interpretations are historicist, yet when Marxist critics adopt a normative attitude toward the literature of the past, they are antihistoricist, as D. W. Fokkema has pointed out.[2] In fact, the choice that the critic has to make is not a simple one between historicism and its antithesis, but one among several possible attitudes, for there are various alternatives to historicism: presentism, historical relativism, perspectivism, and transhistoricism. With regard to the interpretation of Chinese literature, the critic has a similar set of attitudes to choose from: Sinocentrism, Eurocentrism, cultural relativism, cultural perspectivism, and transculturism. By the way, I am avoiding the term "cultural chauvinism" or "ethnocentrism," so that the critic's own cultural and ethnic identity need not be called into question.

The problem about historicism and its various alternatives is complicated by two factors: first, there is some confusion in terminology, and second, disputes about historicism involve both interpretation and evaluation. With regard to terminology, "historicism" is confused with "historical relativism." For instance, Erich Auerbach, in defending historicism and criticizing René Wellek, used the two terms interchangeably, and, what is more surprising, apparently equated both with "perspectivism" when he wrote, "it is wrong to believe that historical relativism or perspectivism makes us incapable of evaluating and judging the work of art, that it leads to arbitrary eclecticism. . . . Historicism is not eclecticism. . . ."[3] Yet it was against the very "perspectivism" espoused by Wellek that Auerbach was arguing! Wellek in his rejoinder to Auerbach likewise made no distinction between "historicism" and "historical relativism."[4] Let us attempt to clarify these and the other terms mentioned above and consider the attitudes these terms denote. Since we are at present concerned only with interpretation and not with evaluation, we shall limit our discussion to the former.

By "historicism" I refer to the attitude that in order to interpret a literary work one must mentally go back to the age in which it was written, and that a work must be interpreted in relation to its historical environment and in terms of the intellectual climate or *Zeitgeist* of its own time.[5] There are some critics, both Chinese and Western, who hold such a historicist attitude. While I can sympathize with their annoyance at anachronisms, false etymologies, and wilful or unwitting distortions of Chinese poetry, and while I share their exasperation at English-speaking readers who prefer their Confucius Pounded, compounded, and confounded, I cannot agree with the historicists all the way, even though my earlier suggestion that in reading one should suspend one's own normal assumptions and beliefs and adopt those of the author or speaker may have led the reader to expect me to be in favor of historicism. Where I differ from the historicists should become clear as our discussion proceeds.

When historicism is applied to the interpretation of Chinese poetry, it naturally becomes concomitant with one form of Sinocentrism. According to this historicist-Sinocentric attitude, we must interpret a poem as the author's contemporary readers presumably would have interpreted it. This leads to several difficulties. In the first place, it is notorious in literary history, Chinese or Western, that an author may be misunderstood by his contemporaries and better understood by posterity. Second, it is questionable whether one can really read a poem as the author's contemporaries would have. At least one cannot *prove* that this is the way they would have read it. Of course, no one denies the necessity of relevant historical knowledge. As Wellek pointed out, no reputable New Critic ever rejected historical knowledge, even though they were antihistoricist.[6] However, to know about a historical period is not the same as having the consciousness of a person who lived in that period. When I said that one should *suspend* one's own assumptions and beliefs and adopt the author's or speaker's, I did not mean that one should *stay* in that situation. The momentary suspension is necessary for *understanding*, but is not sufficient for *interpretation*. Now, any reader acquainted with hermeneutics would immediately sense the presence of the hermeneutical circle, which I shall deal with later. For the present, let me reiterate that we need historical knowledge and imagination to enter the world created by the author in his work, but having done so we need to come back to our own world. Even such an avowed historicist as Roy Harvey Pearce recognized that the world realized for us by a literary work is not the real past world that existed but a possible world that could have existed.[7]

Diametrically opposed to historicism is "presentism" or "presenti-centrism,"[8] according to which a literary work should be interpreted from the point of view of the present. Applied to Chinese poetry, presentism can be concomitant either with Sinocentrism or with Euro-centrism. Presentist-Sinocentrism is aptly summed up by the dictum "Let the past serve the present, let the foreign serve the Chinese" (*gu wei jin yong, yang wei zhong yong*). This also leads to some difficulties. Even if we are willing to accept anachronisms and distortions, and follow our colleagues in China, we cannot always be sure what the current orthodox interpretation of a work may be, or what it will be tomorrow, since orthodox interpretations may change overnight. For example, during the Anti-Confucius campaign, Li Shangyin was praised as an anti-Confucian Legalist. Now that this campaign is over, presumably Li Shangyin need no longer be called a Legalist.

When presentism is concomitant with Eurocentrism, then Chinese literature is interpreted from a modern Western point of view, and in terms of Western genres, conventions, and literary movements. Although few critics have openly proclaimed this attitude, as J. D.

Frodsham did,[9] many have, consciously or otherwise, adopted it in practice, when they have used such terms as "comedy," "plot," or "romanticism." It is this attitude that led critics to deplore the absence of epic and tragedy in Chinese and to lament the "limitations of Chinese fiction." Underlying this attitude is the assumption that the same categories, norms, and conventions apply to both Western and Chinese literature, and that both may therefore be interpreted the same way. Hence we find Freudian, archetypal, and semiotic interpretations of Chinese poetry. I am not totally opposed to the application of modern Western critical methods to Chinese poetry; after all, I was one of the first to try it. What I am pleading for is a judicious examination of the degree of applicability of any critical method to Chinese poetry, as well as its potential fruitfulness. It is possible to write a long analysis of a Chinese poem without making any factual errors but without shedding any light on it either. Also, terminology should be carefully examined before being applied to Chinese literature. For instance, what are sometimes called "archetypes" have not been demonstrated to be universal in all human cultures, but only common in Chinese literature; they should therefore be called cultural constants or common *topoi* rather than "archetypes."

Historical relativism, as I understand it, refers to the attitude that there can be no absolute criteria for validity in interpretation and that each age can interpret a literary work in its own terms and from its own point of view. Historical relativism differs from both historicism and presentism in that it does not claim privileged status for the interpretation of any given age. When this attitude is applied to interlingual and intercultural interpretation, then it can be called cultural relativism. This concept of cultural relativism is not quite the same as D. W. Fokkema's, which is more concerned with evaluation than interpretation and will therefore be discussed in the next chapter. Meanwhile, I wish to point out that although historical relativism is preferable to dogmatic historicism or presentism, it is still not satisfactory, for its amounts to saying, "Your guess is as good as mine," in which case all interpretations are equally valid or invalid. Indeed, the extreme form of relativism is what E. D. Hirsch has called "cognitive atheism,"[10] according to which no one can really understand the past, and all interpretations are "fiction" in disguise. This suicidal attitude, fashionable though it may be in certain circles, is clearly untenable, as suggested by the very fact that those who hold such an attitude still bother to write, just as the fact that Sartre bothered to write the play *Huis Clos* to show the impossibility of interpersonal communication belies the thesis of the play.

Next we shall consider "perspectivism," which is the name given by René Wellek to his belief that in interpreting a literary work one should refer to the values of its own time as well as those of all subsequent periods.[11] Wellek has argued against historicism in these terms: "Asking us to interpret *Hamlet* only in terms of what the very hypothetical views of Shakespeare or his audience were is asking us to forget three hundred years of history. It prohibits us to use the insights of a Goethe or a Coleridge, it impoverishes a work which has attracted and accumulated meanings in the course of history."[12] This is admirably said. However, as D. W. Fokkema realized, perspectivism assumes a linear development of literature in a given culture but will raise problems if applied to intercultural interpretation.[13] Theoretically, we could develop a kind of "cultural perspectivism," which would take into account not only what native critics have said about a literary work but also what non-native critics have said. As a matter of fact, something of this sort has been practiced for some time; I refer to the fact that some Western scholars of Chinese literature have relied heavily on the opinions of Japanese scholars, so much so that a Chinese critic writing in English about Chinese literature will be taken to task for failing to mention all the Japanese works on the subject, although it seems unlikely that if an American or English critic were to write in Chinese about Shakespeare he would be taken to task for failing to mention A. W. Schlegel, W. H. Clemen, M. M. Morozov, and Jan Kott. Anyway, unless and until we have works on Chinese literature in all the major languages of the world, it is unrealistic to speak of cultural perspectivism.

In the light of the above discussion, I see no alternative to transhistoricism and transculturism, by which I do not mean the discovery of absolute and unchanging principles but the search for common denominators, namely, literary features, qualities, functions, and effects that transcend historical and cultural differences. Such common denominators must exist, for otherwise no interpretation would be possible. My belief in the possibility of transhistorical and transcultural interpretation is ultimately based on the simple fact that all authors and readers are human beings who inhabit the same planet earth. To deny the possibility of transhistorical and transcultural interpretation is to be content with living in an isolated here and now, cut off from history and the rest of humanity.

Although Wellek did not use the terms "transhistoricism" and "transculturism," his basic stand appears similar, for he declares:

> There is a common humanity which makes every art remote in time and place, and originally serving functions quite different from aesthetic contemplation, accessible and enjoyable to us. We have risen above the limitations of traditional Western taste—the parochialism and relativism of such taste—into a realm if not of absolute then of universal art.[14]

One can further argue that transhistorical and transcultural interpretation is possible because, as Paul Ricoeur has shown, once discourse is written down, it transcends the original dialogical situation and acquires a certain degree of semantic autonomy and is therefore intelligible to any competent reader.[15] This statement does not contradict the suggestion I made in chapter 2 that the reader "re-means" what the author meant, because there is a dialectic relation between authorial meaning and textual meaning (or between "utterer's meaning" and "utterance's meaning" in Ricoeur's terminology), and between *langue* and *parole*.[16] The textual meaning is the result of the author's act of meaning, since it is the author who chooses the words and puts them together in a particular way. But as soon as the words are written, they function in relation to each other as part of the system of the language as a whole (*langue*), and the author cannot arbitrarily make words mean whatever he wishes, *pace* Humpty Dumpty. Thus a competent reader, relying on his knowledge of the language as *langue*, can understand the textual meaning, thereby repeating the author's act of meaning as *parole*.

My belief in the possibility of transhistorical and transcultural interpretation is further confirmed from an unexpected quarter: Hans Robert Jauss, writing on "The Alterity and Modernity of Medieval Literature," remarks that consciousness of the otherness of the world of medieval literature cannot in itself be the absolute goal of understanding, and continues: "In passing through the surprise of otherness, its possible meaning for us must be sought: the question of a significance which reaches further historically, which surpasses the original communicative situation, must be posed."[17] If the world of medieval

European literature seems "other" to a modern Western reader, how much more so must be the world of classical Chinese poetry! Yet despite this otherness, Chinese poetry can be made meaningful and significant to a modern Western reader, and it is the task of the interlingual critic as interpreter to do so.

Some of the various attitudes mentioned above can be reconciled to some extent if we recognize two stages of interpretation: the first stage mainly concerned with the explication of the "meaning" of a poem, the second with the demonstration of "significance." Although I do not agree with E. D. Hirsch that "meaning" is an intentional object, I still think the distinction between "meaning" and "significance" as summed up by him a useful one: *"Meaning* is that which is represented by a text: it is what the author meant by his use of a particular sequence of signs; it is what the signs represent. *Significance*, on the other hand, names a relationship between that meaning, and a person, or a conception, or indeed anything imaginable."[18] In his earlier book, *Validity in Interpretation*, Hirsch limited the concern of "interpretation" strictly to "meaning," while relegating the concern with "significance" to what he then called "criticism," but in his later book, *The Aims of Interpretation*, he appears to have accepted the concern with significance as part of interpretation, for he writes,

> The public side of interpretation—the *ars explicandi*—is obviously not a monolithic enterprise. It includes not only what biblical scholars have called *interpretatio*, but also what they have traditionally called *applicatio* (significance). Interpretation includes both functions whenever it answers both the question, What does this text mean?, and also the question, What use or value does it have: how is its meaning applied to me, to us, in our particular situation? . . . The chief value of interpretation is found in this *applicatio*, not in pure *interpretatio* alone.[19]

My "first stage" of interpretation, then, corresponds to *interpretatio*, and my "second stage" to *applicatio*. In interpreting a Chinese poem, during the first stage of interpretation, the interlingual critic is concerned with explaining what he believes the author meant by the words of the poem. To do so he needs all the historical and philological knowledge he can get, for he has to explain not only the semantic, syntactic, prosodic, rhetorical, and stylistic features of the poem but also historical and literary allusions and cultural backgrounds. He has to show how a poet, who had to take into account not only linguistic rules but also literary conventions, performed his individual act of meaning and creating. Of course, a poet may transcend linguistic and literary conventions, but he cannot totally ignore them. It is the critic's task to demonstrate how a poet has observed, or modified, or transcended the linguistic and literary conventions of his day to create an imaginary world in a linguistic structure. Further, the critic needs to display this world in all its "otherness" to his own reader, and to do this he needs to be familiar with the cultural world in which the world of the poem was born. I hope that by now it is clear that I am not antihistorical or ahistorical, but simply wish to go a step beyond historicism.

On the other hand, the critic also needs to show his reader how, in spite of its apparent "otherness," the world of a Chinese poem does have something in common with the reader's own world. It is the critic's duty to point out and enlarge the area of intersection between the world of the poem and that of the reader; for I believe that we read poetry in order to understand better the world we live in and to enrich our lives, but we do not live in order to read poetry. The modern Western reader of Chinese poetry, whether in the original or in translation, should be made aware that Chinese poetry is not an exotic object, of antiquarian interest only, but something alive that has important things to say to him about the world in which he lives. Unlike some Western Sinologists who apparently think that classical Chinese poetry should be treated like King Tut's treasures, to be kept in a museum and admired from a distance but not touched, I wish Chinese poetry to be read, handled, and loved as a living presence.

During the second stage of interpretation, it is legitimate, I think, to use modern terminology, of which the original author had no knowledge. This does not constitute anachronism, of which I have been accused, for it is one thing to attribute to an ancient author ideas and beliefs that he could not possibly have entertained, but quite another to describe in one's own terms what he wrote. For instance, it would be anachronistic to say that Du Fu had "democratic" or "antifeudal" ideas, for even though he expressed indignation at social injustice and political corruption, he did not question the whole political system under which he lived. However, it would not be anachronistic to say that Li He expressed feelings that we would now characterize as "paranoiac," even though he could not have known the term, just as it would not be anachronistic to say Sima Xiangru suffered from diabetes, even though he could not have known the term. If we had to interpret an ancient author in the terminology of his own time, then we would have to describe the measurements of a Zhou bronze vessel not in centimeters or inches but in Zhou *chi*. As a matter of fact, interpretation by its very nature entails "translating" (even if in the same language) an author's terms into different terms. Otherwise all interpretations would be either impossible or tautological. I once heard (from whom I cannot recall) that when T. S. Eliot was asked what he meant by "Lady, three white leopards sat under a juniper-tree," he replied by simply repeating the line. Now Eliot the poet had the privilege to do so, but Eliot the critic could hardly have, let alone any critic who is not also a major poet in his own right.

Lest there be any misunderstanding, I hasten to add that in justifying the use of modern terminology in the interpretation of classical Chinese poetry, I am not condoning the practice of reading into Chinese poems wildly improbable ideas and ubiquitous Freudian symbols. Freudian interpretations, often based on false etymology and far-fetched associations of ideas, tell us more about the obsessions of the interpreters than the texts they are supposed to interpret. The same is true, to a lesser extent perhaps, of allegorical interpretations. I do not deny that there was an allegorical tradition in Confucian hermeneutics, or that Chinese poets sometimes did write allegorically, but it is absurd to interpret every poem as political or moral allegory. Even if a poet did have an allegorical *meaning* in mind, we can still interpret the *significance* of the poem in universal and symbolic terms rather than local and allegorical terms. Or, to borrow Dante's terminology, we may interpret a poem on the allegorical (i.e., worldly symbolic) level or the anagogical (i.e., other-worldly) level, rather than on the tropological (i.e., personal and moral) level. For example, Li Shangyin's famous couplet

夕陽無限好
只是近黃昏

xi yang wu xian hao
evening sun no limit good

zhi shi jin huanghun
only is near yellow-twilight[20]

The setting sun is of infinite beauty—
Only, the time is approaching nightfall[21]

has been interpreted allegorically as a prophetic reference to the fall
of the Tang dynasty. Apart from the question whether the poet really
was a political prophet, it is surely permissible to read the couplet as
an expression of universal truths: that the awareness that something
beautiful will soon vanish heightens one's perception of its beauty and
one's enjoyment of it, that the extreme of joy leads to sorrow, that all
beauty is transient in this world. This reading does not necessarily
exclude the allegorical one but extends the significance of the poem.[22]

Both Freudian interpretations and allegorical ones, either separately
or together, are often combined with the biographical approach to literature, with the result that every literary work of art is reduced to a
roman à clef. Much ingenuity and labor have been squandered on
some Chinese literary works, notably Li Shangyin's ambiguous poems
and the novel *A Red Mansion Dream*, with regard to the possible
identities of the supposed prototypes of the persons mentioned in
these works, just as in the West much ingenuity and labor have been
squandered on the identity of the Dark Lady of Shakespeare's sonnets
and that of the mysterious lover in Emily Dickinson's poems. In their
eagerness to identify every person or even object in a literary work
with an actual historical person, critics inclined to the biographical
and allegorical modes of interpretation are apt to forget that they are
dealing with literary works of art and that even in the case of a *roman
à clef* its literary merits, if any, do not depend on the identities of the
prototypes of its fictitious characters. Fascinating as it may be, literary
detection has little to offer to literary interpretation and remains outside the scope of literary criticism.

It is not my intention to suggest that there is only one single correct
approach to Chinese poetry, or one single correct method of interpretation, for I am well aware that the mode of interpretation often depends on the nature of the work to be interpreted. Neither is it my
intention to launch a systematic attack on any particular school of
criticism or interpretation. Nonetheless, it remains a fact that some

approaches to literature and some methods of interpretation are less valid and less fruitful than others. I simply wish to point out some of the more egregious dangers of misinterpretation.

So far we have not yet faced the problem of the hermeneutical circle, which can be described in terms of the interrelation between "understanding" and "explanation," or in terms of that between "parts" and "whole." To put it as simply as possible: in order to understand a text, one must explain it, yet in order to explain it, one must understand it. Alternatively, one can only understand the whole text from its constituent parts, yet the parts only make sense as parts of the whole. This seemingly vicious circle, as Hirsch and Ricoeur have shown, is in fact breakable. The dialectic between understanding and explanation has been summed up by Ricoeur in these words:

> I propose to describe this dialectic first as a move from understanding to explaining and then as a move from explanation to comprehension. The first time, understanding will be a naive grasping of the meaning of the text as a whole. The second time, comprehension will be a sophisticated mode of understanding, supported by explanatory procedures.[23]

To put it slightly differently, as I suggested in chapter 1, the hermeneutical circle can be turned into an open-ended spiral of infinite reinterpretations, for we can continue to modify and refine the initial understanding with new knowledge gained from explanatory procedures. Whether we adopt this metaphor of the spiral or use the term that Hirsch borrowed from Jean Piaget, "corrigible schemata,"[24] the interpretive process remains the same, and when a critic is reasonably satisfied with the level of understanding he has reached, he may share it with his readers, without claiming that what he offers is the definitive interpretation.

How the hermeneutical spiral, if I may now so term it, operates with regard to the interpretation of classical Chinese poetry can be easily illustrated. In reading Chinese poetry in traditional editions, which are unpunctuated and in which poems are not printed in separate lines but as whole texts, it is quite possible, even for an experienced reader, to make a mistake about the meter of the poem, such as mistaking a heptasyllabic poem for a pentasyllabic one. Take one of Du Fu's lesser-known poems, entitled

蘇端薛復筵簡薛華醉歌

Su Duan Xue Fu yan jian Xue Hua zui ge.[25]

Even the title causes some problems. At first sight it appears to mean, "At Su Duan's and Xue Fu's banquet, note to Xue Hua, drunken song," or, in other words, "At a banquet given by Su Duan and Xue Fu, I send this drunken song in lieu of a note to Xue Hua." However, when we read the text of the poem, we encounter these lines:

座中薛華善醉歌
歌詞自作風格老

zuo zhong Xue Hua shan zui ge
seat amid Xue Hua excel drunk song
ge ci zi zuo feng'ge lao
song word self make style old

Among those seated, Xue Hua excels in drunken songs,
The song-words he composes himself, their style mature.

Now it seems that it was Xue Hua who wrote a drunken song at the banquet, so that the title should be understood to mean, "A poetic note to Xue Hua, who wrote a drunken song at the banquet given by Su Duan and Xue Fu." Yet the possibility that the present poem is another "drunken song" that Du Fu wrote after the banquet and then sent to Xue Hua, as one commentator suggested,[26] cannot be excluded, so that the title can also be taken to mean, "A drunken song sent in lieu of a note to Xue Hua [who also wrote a drunken song] at the banquet given by Su Duan and Xue Fu." So much for the title. When we come to the text of the poem itself, it is quite possible to take the first five syllables as a line:

文章有神交

wen zhang you shen jiao
literary composition has spiritual communion

More freely, "In literature, there is a spiritual communion," which makes good sense. But when one goes on to the next five syllables,

有道端復得

you dao duan fu de
have way proper again get

they do not make good sense. So one goes back to the beginning and takes the first *seven* syllables as a line:

文章有神交有道

wen zhang you shen jiao you dao
literary composition has spirit, communion has way

and realizes that this means, "In literary compositions, there is spirit; in communion [or friendship] there is a Way." The next seven syllables make a satisfactory second line:

端復得之名譽早

Duan Fu de zhi ming yu zao
Duan Fu get it fame reputation early

One now realizes that the characters *duan* and *fu* are the personal names of the two hosts mentioned in the title (rather than words meaning "proper" and "again"), and that the second line means, "Duan and Fu have obtained these, and so enjoyed early fame." In the light of this, the first line now appears not to be a general statement but a compliment to Duan and Fu and should be understood as, "In their literary compositions, there is spirit; in making friends, they have the Way." Thus, we have arrived at a better understanding than the initial one.

In reading lyrical meters *(ci)*, which have highly complex tone patterns and rhyme schemes, unless one is familiar with the metrical pattern named after a musical tune, one can only form a general understanding by following the syntax and rhymes. It is only with the help of a manual of lyrical meters *(cipu)* that one can arrive at a more definite understanding. Yet the compilers of such manuals only established the "standard" patterns inductively from extant specimens and not deductively from a priori knowledge of the actual musical tunes. This is another illustration of the hermeneutical spiral, of the dialectic between understanding and explanation.

To conclude this chapter: I believe that the interlingual critic of Chinese poetry should aspire to be transhistorical and transcultural, without minimizing the historical and cultural differences between Chinese poetry and Western poetry. He should demonstrate both the similarity of the world of a Chinese poem to the reader's world and its alterity, for it is the similarity that enables the reader to share the world of the poem, and it is the alterity that enables him to extend his own world. The critic should not, in his search for archetypes, symbols, structural patterns, and what not, lose sight of the unique world of each poem, which is the concrete embodiment of some universal human experience or abstract idea, but should try to see how the unique world of the poem emerges from its unique linguistic structure. Furthermore, he should show not only *what* a Chinese poem is like but also *why* it is worth reading. This leads to the question of evaluation, with which the next chapter will be concerned.

5

The Critic as Arbiter

B Y "ARBITER" here I do not mean *arbiter elegantiae* but one who makes value judgments on literary works. As already suggested in the introduction, interpretation necessarily entails evaluation, because the cognition of a work of art always involves value judgment, as theorists from Kant to Wellek and Hirsch have pointed out. Since I have neither the competence nor the inclination to discuss problems of axiology on the theoretical level, I shall simply try to answer the practical question: by what, and whose, criteria should an interlingual critic evaluate a Chinese poem? By the author's own, if these are known? By those of the author's contemporaries? By those of later Chinese critics? And if so, which ones? By those of our contemporaries in China? By those of some school of modern Western criticism? And if so, which? The critic can choose from the same set of possible attitudes as mentioned in the preceding chapter, but there is no need to go over all of them again one by one, for the arguments advanced against historicism, presentism, Sinocentrism, Eurocentrism, and extreme relativism with regard to interpretation can also apply to evaluation. However, there is one attitude, the kind of cultural relativism advocated by D. W. Fokkema, that deserves some consideration. Fokkema defined "cultural relativism" as follows:

> by cultural relativism one might understand an approach, which interprets the literary-historical phenomena of a certain period within a certain cultural area and evaluates them on the basis of the norms and against the background of that period and that cultural area, and which

further compares the different value systems underlying the various periods and cultural areas.[1]

This is certainly an unobjectionable attitude, but one cannot help wondering what happens after the critic has compared the different value systems. Would he not have to choose among them? And how would the knowledge that these different value systems are relative help him in dealing with an individual work or author? I am afraid that, as Wellek put it, "there is simply no way of avoiding judgment by us, by myself."[2] However, this does not mean that all value judgments are purely subjective and arbitrary. It is possible, I believe, to aim at transcultural and transhistorical evaluation, which does not mean the establishment and application of any single, universal, absolute, and inflexible criterion or set of criteria, but the search for poetically valuable qualities that are not limited to any particular language, or culture, or period. And by "poetically valuable qualities" I do not mean anything as vague as "organic unity," or "significant form," or "tension," but qualities that can be demonstrated as contributing to the success of the work as a whole. I should further make clear that I am using the term "poetically valuable qualities" to include both what Ingarden calls "artistic value qualities" and "aesthetic value qualities." Ingarden makes a distinction between "artistic value" and "aesthetic value": the former "is something which arises in the work of art itself and has its existential ground in that"; the latter "is something which manifests itself only in the aesthetic object and at a particular moment which determines the character of the whole."[3] As examples of artistic value qualities, he mentions such qualities as "clarity" and "order," and as examples of aesthetic value qualities, he mentions "pathetic," "sublime," "witty," "interesting," "boring," and others.[4] Although I recognize the validity of the distinction between "artistic values" and "aesthetic values" and that between "artistic value qualities" and "aesthetic value qualities" in theory, I am not maintaining the distinction in practice, for the following reasons.

In the first place, certain qualities that are relevant to artistic values, such as "clarity," "obscurity," "simplicity," and "complexity," are by no means universally positive qualities but may be either positive or negative in value, depending on the work in which they are present and the part they play in it. Second, it is difficult to draw a strict line between "artistic value qualities" and "aesthetic value qualities" in practice. For example, if, in talking about a poem, we say, "the tonal pattern is perfect," or "this is a false rhyme," we are talking about its "artistic value qualities," but as soon as we say, "the tonal pattern has an exhilarating effect," we are talking about its "aesthetic value qualities." Furthermore, aesthetic value qualities such as "interesting" and "boring" can have no objective criteria: what is "boring" to some readers may be "exciting" to others. Basically, the distinction between "artistic values" and "aesthetic values" and that between "artistic value qualities" and "aesthetic value qualities" are derived from the distinction between "work of art" and "aesthetic object." The former exists independently of any observer, although in a potential state, whereas the latter only comes into existence when perceived by an observer. The distinction is necessary for analytical purposes, but in practice it is difficult to talk about a poem as a "work of art" without at the same time talking about it as an "aesthetic object," since one can only know the poem qua "work of art" through one's own concretization of it qua "aesthetic object," However, I realize that it is possible to recognize the artistic value qualities of a work without liking it. In this connection it is useful to consider Mikel Dufrenne's distinction between "taste" and "tastes." According to Dufrenne, to have "taste" means "to possess the capacity of judgment which is beyond prejudice and partisanship," whereas to have "tastes" means to have arbitrary preferences.[5] To avoid confusion, perhaps we can write the former with a capital T as "Taste," and the latter as "tastes," or call the former "discrimination" and the latter "preference." I would not go as far as Dufrenne, who asserted that "to have taste is to have no tastes,"[6] for surely even the most discriminating critic is still entitled to have his personal preferences. To me the distinction between "Taste" and "tastes" is that the former refers to the ability to distinguish between what is good and what is bad among things of the same kind, and the latter refers to preference of one kind of thing to another. Take cuisine as an illustration. One cannot argue whether Chinese cuisine or French cuisine is superior, and one has every right to prefer either, but a gourmet should be able to distinguish between superior and inferior Chinese cooking or between superior and inferior French cooking. What is more, between superior Chinese cuisine and superior French cuisine there are qualities in common, which can be discussed in terms of balance, temperature, timing, texture, and so on, and there are qualities that are desirable irrespective of the style of cooking: for example, meat should be tender rather than tough, deep fried food should be crisp rather than soggy, soup should be either hot or cold rather than lukewarm, and so on. A critic of poetry should have Taste, but this does not stop him having personal tastes. He should be able to recognize artistic values even if he does not enjoy them personally. It is comparable to recognizing a person's physical beauty without feeling sexually attracted.

One should also realize that the artistic and aesthetic values of a poem are not to be confused with its possible emotional impact on a reader. The critic should describe qualities that are artistically and aesthetically valuable in a poem, not his own mental state induced by reading it. To say that a poem is "deeply moving" or that "it moved me to tears" is not to prove its artistic and aesthetic excellence, since one can be moved to tears by a child's scribbles saying "I miss you," which does not prove that the child has written a good poem. Nor is it sufficient to recognize, as R. G. Collingwood pointed out, that a work of art *expresses* emotions rather than *arouses* them,[7] for there are other effective ways of expressing emotions than artistic ones. To kiss someone is perhaps a more effective way of expressing one's love than to write a love poem, and to slap someone on the face is at least as effective a way of expressing one's anger as writing a satire. When we say that a poem is "moving" or that it makes us feel certain emotions such as anger or pity, what we really mean is that it makes us feel *as if* we were experiencing such emotions, or, in other words, it makes us *imagine* that we are undergoing such emotions. To fail to distinguish between actually experiencing certain emotions and imagining them is to behave like the legendary old lady who, while watching the final scene of *Hamlet,* loudly warned the Prince that Laertes' sword was poisoned.

Two other qualities that have often been taken as universal criteria for poetic excellence but in fact cannot be so taken are "originality" and "sincerity." Modern critics, both Western ones and Chinese ones influenced by Western literary criticism, are especially prone to use the former as a criterion, and Chinese critics rooted in traditional criticism are especially prone to use the latter. Let us consider "originality" first.

To begin with, "originality" should not be confused with "creativity." The former means doing something that has never been done before or doing it in a way that has never been done before, whereas the latter means producing something that did not exist before. Thus, if I write a poem that is not identical with any previously existing poem, then my poem is "creative," even if the words, images, rhythms, and so on in the poem are quite conventional and not original. Modern critics tend to regard "originality" in the sense of "novelty" as a sure indication of artistic excellence, under the mistaken notion that only what is "original" is truly "creative." In fact, originality is not synonymous with excellence. It is perfectly possible to produce something totally original but artistically and aesthetically valueless. For instance, I could write a line that nobody has written before, such as *shan shan shan shan shan* ("mountain, mountain, mountain, mountain, mountain"), which would be truly original, but would it be good poetry? Of course, such a line *could* become good poetry if given an appropriate context, like Shakespeare's "No, no, no, no" or "Never, never, never, never, never" in *King Lear*, but that is not the point at issue.

Second, as T. S. Eliot remarked, "in poetry there is no such thing as complete originality owing nothing to the past."[8] This is particularly true with regard to classical Chinese poetry, which has had a long tradition and has been written by poets deeply conscious of that tradition, even if some of them rebelled against it. In classical Chinese poetry, we cannot expect to find absolute originality, but originality of a kind that I have elsewhere called "kaleidoscopic,"[9] in the sense that the words, phrases, images, and the like in a poem may be conventional, but the pattern that emerges from the way the poet has combined them is different from any previously existing one.

Traditional Chinese poets and critics had different opinions about originality. Some advocated originality and warned against clichés. To mention the two most famous examples: Du Fu wrote, "If my words do not astonish people, I would not stop even after death,"[10] and Han Yu wrote, "Stale words must be removed."[11] Among later critics, Zhao Yi (1727–1814) praised Du Fu, Han Yu, and other poets for their originality in syntax, verse form, or prosody, and emphasized novelty instead of imitation of ancient poets.[12] In contrast, poets and critics whom I have called "archaists," such as Huang Tingjian (1045–1105), advocated imitating earlier poets and observing prosodic rules.[13] Actually, the disputes between the archaists and their opponents often centered on the question of individuality rather than originality. Those who opposed archaism, such as the Yuan brothers of the Gongan School, namely, Yuan Zongdao (1560–1600), Yuan Hongdao (1568–1610), and Yuan Zhongdao (1570–1623), insisted that one should express one's own personality in writing and speak with one's own voice, rather than that one should write in a totally original manner.[14] Once we realize the distinction between "originality" and "individuality," we shall no longer feel obliged to regard the former as a sine qua non of good poetry or to consider the lack of originality as equivalent to the absence of individuality. I do not mean that originality is of no importance in the evaluation of poetry, only that it is not an absolute criterion.

If an "original" poem is not necessarily a good one, by the same token a poem that is "imitative" or "derivative" is not ipso facto a bad one, but should be judged on its own merits, whether the poet was consciously imitating an earlier poet or unconsciously "echoing" an earlier one. Consider the following poem:

竹裏

竹裏編茅倚石根
竹莖疎處見前村
閒眠盡日無人到
自有春風爲掃門

Zhu-li
Bamboo-inside
zhu-li bian mao yi shi-gen
bamboo-inside weave thatch lean rock-root
zhu jing shu chu jian qian cun
bamboo stalk spare place see front village
xian mian jin ri wu ren dao
leisurely sleep all day no person arrive
zi you chun feng wei sao men
self have spring wind for sweep door

Amidst Bamboos
Amidst bamboos I built a thatched hut against the rocks,

Where the bamboo stalks are sparse, I see the village in
    front.
Lying at ease all day—no one comes here—
I have the spring wind to sweep the door for me.

This poem was included by Li Bi (1159–1222)[15] in his annotated edition of the collected poems of Wang Anshi (1021–86) and accepted as
Wang's work by later editors and commentators.[16] However, in 1957
Qian Zhongshu (Ch'ien Chung-shu), in the introduction to his *Annotated Selections of Song Poetry* (*Song shi xuanzhu*), pointed out that
the poem was really by the Buddhist monk Xianzhong, and Wang
only inscribed it on a wall.[17] Li Bi also pointed out the similarity of
this poem to another poem by He Zhu (1063–1120) and quoted an
apocryphal anecdote about Wang's supposed admiration of He's poem.
But Qian Zhongshu argued that He Zhu's poem in question was written three years after he had lamented Wang Anshi's death, so Wang
could not possibly have seen it.[18] On the other hand, since we are not
certain that He Zhu knew the poem by Monk Xianzhong, we shall
not discuss the question whether the former was influenced by the
latter. Instead, we shall compare Xianzhong's poem with a much
earlier one, by Wang Wei:

竹里館

獨坐幽篁裏

彈琴復長嘯

深林人不知

明月來相照

Zhu-li Guan
Bamboo-lane Cottage
du zuo you huang li
alone sit secluded bamboo inside
tan qin fu chang xiao
pluck zither again long whistle
shen lin ren bu zhi
deep grove people not know
ming yue lai xiang zhao
bright moon come (one) shine[19]

Cottage in Bamboo-lane
Sitting alone amidst secluded bamboos,

I play the zither, then utter a long whistle.
Deep in the grove, unknown to people—
The bright moon comes to shine upon one.

It should be explained that "whistle" (*xiao*) is associated with Taoist breath-control exercises and does not have the same connotations as the word "whistle" does in modern English, and that the word *xiang*, which sometimes means "mutually," here simply indicates that the verb *zhao* ("shine") has an unidentified object.

It is obvious that even the title of Monk Xianzhong's poem is reminiscent of Wang Wei's,[20] and this could hardly be a coincidence, since Wang's poem has always been extremely well known. However, I believe that Xianzhong was not copying Wang Wei in a mechanical fashion, nor was he trying to forget, and make his reader forget, Wang Wei's poem. He was writing his own poem with Wang Wei's poem at the back of his mind, and he knew that when his reader should recall Wang's poem, which he almost inevitably would, it would add a further dimension to the present poem, not diminish it. If Xianzhong's poem is less satisfactory than Wang Wei's, it is not because it is imitative or derivative, but because it is less concise and less free from self-consciousness. Compare the last lines of the two poems: whereas Wang Wei simply says, "The bright moon comes to shine on one," Xianzhong says, "I myself [or "naturally," the word *zi* meaning both "self" and "naturally"] have the spring wind to sweep the door *for* [me]." The use of the words *zi* and *wei* ("for") suggests a self-conscious relationship with Nature, whereas Wang Wei's poem presents a world in which Self is totally absorbed in Nature. One can argue that a totally unselfconscious attitude to Nature is not necessarily the most desirable attitude, but that is not the point at issue. The point is that Xianzhong was presumably trying to present the same kind of world and attitude to Nature that Wang Wei did, and was less successful. Another poet with a different attitude to Nature should, of course, be judged on other grounds.

While we are still on the subject of originality, I may add that the question of originality or innovation assumes greater importance when we are assessing a poet's position in literary history than when we are evaluating his poetry synchronically against the works of other poets of different periods. A poet like Shen Yue (441–513), who initiated prosodic rules that led to the establishment of Regulated Verse, is obviously more important in literary history than as a poet in his own right, side by side with the major Tang poets. This is but another confirmation of the distinction between literary history and literary criticism. However, I certainly do not wish to divorce literary criticism from literary history or scholarship. In fact, I think the separation of "literary criticism" from "literary scholarship" is unfortunate, since a critic without scholarship is a dilettante, and a scholar without critical discernment is a hack. All I wish to suggest is that one should be aware of which role one is playing at a given moment.

To turn to "sincerity": this has often been used as a criterion for evaluating poetry by critics who hold expressive views of literature, both Chinese and Western, both ancient and modern. Two underlying assumptions can be discerned here: first, that emotional impact is equivalent to poetic excellence, and second, that in order to produce the emotional impact, the author must feel the emotion himself. The first assumption we have already seen to be untrue. The second assumption, which in Western criticism was neatly summed up by Horace's formulation "si vis me flere, dolendum est / Primum ipsi tibi" ("If you would have me weep, you must first show grief yourself") and echoed by others, as M. H. Abrams has shown,[21] is actually no more tenable than the first assumption. For one thing, we have no independent sources of information to prove or disprove whether a poet really felt the emotion that he professes to feel in a poem. Even when we do have what may seem to be independent sources of information, such as the poet's own letters and journals or those of his relatives and friends, these still cannot be used as evidence of his sincerity or insincerity. The letter from Li Shangyin to his future patron that I quoted in chapter 2 can help us *understand* the poem written about the same time,[22] but cannot prove the poet's sincerity in the poem, for he could have been just as insincere in the letter as in the poem. To use a Western example: the case of Pushkin mentioned by Victor Erlich is instructive.[23] While idealizing a certain Mrs. K. in a poem, Pushkin was writing about her in almost obscene terms in a letter to a friend; yet the letter does not necessarily prove that the poem is insincere, only that Pushkin was following different conventions when writing in different genres. Similarly, when Ouyang Xiu (1007–72) wrote official history or formal essays on political and philosophical subjects, he adopted a high moral tone, but when he wrote lyrics (*ci*), he adopted a romantic and at times even erotic tone.[24] This does not prove that he was either a moral hypocrite or an insincere lover; he was simply playing different roles. The fact is that when we say that a poet is "sincere," we really mean that he is *convincing*, which only goes to show how good a writer he is, just as the would-be dreamer I invented in chapter 1 is convincing to the extent of his ability to describe his dream. Thus, to use sincerity of emotion as a criterion for poetic excellence is to put the cart before the horse, for it is artistic skill that produces the impression of sincerity, not sincerity that produces artistic excellence.

We have seen that qualities that may seem to be poetically valuable, such as clarity and complexity, are not necessarily so. Conversely, qualities that may seem to be neutral may turn out to be axiologically relevant. For example, it would be absurd to claim that a pentasyllabic Quatrain is necessarily superior to a heptasyllabic one, yet in the case of Wang Wei's poem compared with Monk Xianzhong's, the fact that the former is a pentasyllabic Quatrain and therefore more concise and implicit, whereas the latter is a heptasyllabic one and therefore less concise and more explicit, is not irrelevant to the relative poetic values of the two poems. To give another example: one cannot attach positive poetic values to any particular phonemes or combination of phonemes, but when a poet uses a sequence of words that combine certain phonemes with certain semantic and syntactic structures, the result is highly relevant to the question of the poem's artistic and aesthetic values.

The above discussions should not lead to the conclusion that there can be no criterion or guideline in evaluating poetry, for though we cannot single out any one quality as the universal criterion for excellence in poetry, we can still, following the general conception of poetry described in chapter 1, identify and analyze qualities that contribute to the poem's success as a poem, or in other words, qualities that help the poem fulfil its artistic function. It is possible to demonstrate how the linguistic structure of a poem enables it to yield a unique world and to satisfy our creative impulse vicariously. This means we can evaluate a poem not according to some arbitrary and rigid criteria but according to a general guideline based on the conception of poetry as the overlapping of linguistic structure and artistic function, the latter being conceived of as extension of reality through the creation (on the author's part) and re-creation (on the reader's part) of imaginary worlds, and satisfaction of the creative impulse for both author and reader.

It should be obvious that this conception of poetry does not limit "poetic" values to strictly aesthetic ones, since "extension of reality" is considered an essential part of the artistic function of poetry. In asking how far a poem extends the reader's perception of reality and what kind of world it yields, we are raising questions of extra-aesthetic values. The world of a poem may be happy or sad, pleasant or horrible, but it cannot be considered valuable if it is trivial or superficial, and as soon as we talk about "triviality" or "superficiality," we are talking about extra-aesthetic values. Nonetheless, aesthetic values and extra-aesthetic values should not be confused. Even a dogmatic critic committed to a certain ideology must admit that two literary works that are equally sound in ideology may not be equally good as literature, and the superiority of the one over the other can only be attributed to superior artistic/aesthetic values. As a human being, every reader or critic has the right to object to a poem on moral, political, social, or personal grounds, but no right to say it is a bad poem on the same grounds, just as a man has the right to refuse to have sexual relations with a beautiful woman because he knows she has V.D., but no right to say she is not beautiful because of it.

To return from the ridiculous to the sublime or at least serious: it may be true that, as E. D. Hirsch has argued, the so-called intrinsic study of literature is really the aesthetic study of literature and no more intrinsic to the nature of literature than any other approach.[25] However, I still think, as does Hirsch himself, that this is the most fruitful and rewarding approach, because it focuses on the literary work itself, without necessarily neglecting its relations to the world, the author, and the reader, whereas some other approaches tend to lead the reader further and further away from the literary work and more and more into realms of sweeping generalizations about anthropology, psychology, history, linguistics, and what not. To be sure, these arc all valuable academic disciplines and branches of human knowledge, but if one is primarily interested in one of these, why should one choose to be a literary critic?

It is perhaps necessary to reaffirm one's belief in the value of literature and that of literary criticism, when there is so much trendish talk about "deconstructioning" literary texts, about the nonexistence of literature, and about the impossibility of interpretaion. Even such an acute critic as George Steiner, whom I greatly admire and with whose views I generally agree, in his recent article "Critic/Reader," while arguing against current negative trends, gratuitously emphasizes the "parasitic" nature of criticism because it is ontologically posterior to art.[26] There is no need to do so, for if criticism is parasitic because it is ontologically posterior to art, then zoology is parasitic because it is ontologically posterior to animals. And the fact that literary critics do not know, or cannot agree about, what exactly literature is should be no more cause for despair than that biologists do not know, or cannot agree about, what exactly life is, and physicists do not know, or cannot agree about, what exactly the physical universe is. However, whereas physicists can happily argue about "quarks" and "gluons" among themselves, literary critics who indulge in their own critical "metalanguages," which are in fact nothing but jargon (or at most "sublanguages," since they still follow the linguistic rules of some "natural language"), will soon find few, if any, willing to listen.

6

A Critical Exercise

IN THE PRECEDING chapters I have translated and discussed various Chinese poems and lines to illustrate points raised concerning theoretical and methodological issues. In the present chapter I wish to focus attention on interrelations between time, space, and self in Chinese poetry. Since even an imaginary world created by a poet must exist in imaginary time and space, an examination of the ways in which the speaker of a poem orients himself to time and space will help us better orient ourselves to the world of that poem, and since such an examination will inevitably involve analysis of various aspects of language, it will also help us understand better how the world of the poem emerges from its linguistic structure. This in turn will help us gauge the extent to which the poet has succeeded in realizing the potentialities of language and thus satisfying his own creative impulse and ours. A study of time-space-self interrelations is therefore relevant to both the interpretation of Chinese poetry and its evaluation. However, a comprehensive and thorough study would require a separate volume: what follows is merely a critical exercise intended to demonstrate the kind of approach that can be derived from the conception of poetry described in the first chapter. I have deliberately chosen as examples poems familiar to all students of Chinese literature so as to show how this approach can throw new light on extremely well-known poems. All examples are in the *shi* genre, but similar examples can be found in other poetic genres.

TIME, SELF, AND DIRECTIONALITY

As already pointed out in chapter 3, although there are no tense inflections in Chinese, "tense" understood as the semantactic category that establishes the relationship between what is spoken of and the time of speaking does exist in Chinese poetry. Some linguists have introduced the concepts of "moving ego" and "moving time" into discussions of tense. Both of these concepts are frequently encountered in Chinese poetry. On the one hand, human life is often compared to a journey; on the other, time is often compared to a flowing river, an arrow, or some other moving object. An investigation into such common expressions properly belongs to linguistics rather than poetics. However, it is interesting to consider the concepts of moving ego and moving time, as they appear in poetry, in conjunction with directionality (which is, of course, one aspect of space). Generally speaking, no matter whether one thinks of oneself as moving, or time as moving, or both, there are only two alternatives in directionality: one is either facing time or facing the same direction as time. This is due to the simple fact that we have eyes in front only; had we eyes, as birds and fish do, on the left and right sides, our whole orientation to space would presumably be quite different. As things are, we are primarily oriented to the space in front, which is therefore called by some linguists "canonical space."[1] And since temporal relations are expressed in spatial terms, apparently in all languages, we normally speak of time as if it were in front of us. However, in Chinese poetry, sometimes the speaker seems to perceive time as being behind, or as moving in the same direction as the speaker. I propose to designate the situation "Confrontation" when the speaker is imagined as facing time, whether he is conceived as static or moving, and whether time is conceived as static or moving; and to designate it "Concurrence" when the speaker is imagined as facing the same direction as time, whether he is conceived as static or moving. It makes no difference whether time is conceived as a straight line (either horizontal or vertical) or as a circle, for in any case one has to face either direction, front or back. (I assume that in the case of circular time one would be on the circumference; if one were at the center, one would no longer be *in* time.)

We shall first look at examples of Confrontation.

1. Ego static, time moving toward ego:

棄我去者昨日之日不可留
亂我心者今日之日多煩擾
　　　（李白，宣州謝朓樓
　　　餞別校書叔雲）

qi wo qu zhe zuori zhi ri bu ke liu
abandon me depart that-which yesterday's day not can detain
luan wo xin zhe jinri zhi ri duo fan you
disturb my heart that-which today's day much worry grief.²

What has abandoned me and departed: the day of yesterday
　　which could not be detained;
What disturbs my heart: the day of today which is full of
　　worry and grief.

> (From Li Bo, "At the Farewell
> Party for Collator Uncle Yun at
> Xie Tiao's Pavilion in Xuanzhou")

These two lines open an otherwise heptasyllabic poem in Ancient Style (*guti*). Their unusual length, together with the repetition of the word *ri* ("day"), suggests an endless succession of days marching past the speaker. The repetition is effected by the unusual structures of *zuori zhi ri* ("yesterday's day") and *jinri zhi ri* ("today's day"), so that instead of saying simply, "What has abandoned me and departed is yesterday; what disturbs my heart is today," the poet says in effect, "What has abandoned me and departed is the day that I now call yesterday; what disturbs my heart is the day that I now call today [but will become yesterday tomorrow]." In this way, emphasis is placed on the idea of "day," with the implication that the words "yesterday" and "today" have shifting referents. Although there is nothing unusual about saying that yesterday has departed, the use of *qu* ("depart") as a full verb instead of a modifier (such as in *qunian*, "last year" or "the year gone by"), together with the personification of "yesterday" suggested by the word *qi* ("abandon"), dramatizes the movement of time and the speaker's inability to stop it. This in itself is sufficient cause for grief, apart from any other causes that "today" may bring. These lines remind one of

> To-morrow, to-morrow, and to-morrow
> Creeps in this petty pace from day to day,³

except that whereas Li Bo, though full of grief, still regrets the fast passage of time, the world-weary Macbeth feels it slowly creeping by. We may also compare Li Bo's lines with Apollinaire's

> Vienne la nuit, sonne l'heure,
> Les jours s'en vont, je demeure.[4]

Here, too, time is moving toward the speaker, and passing him by, while he stays where he is, motionless and helpless.

2. Ego moving forward, time static:

君問歸期未有期
巴山夜雨漲秋池
何當共剪西窗燭
卻話巴山夜雨時

（李商隱，夜雨寄北）

jun wen gui qi wei you qi
you ask return date not-yet have date
Bashan ye yu zhang qiu chi
Ba-mountain night rain swell autumn pond
he dang gong jian xi chuang zhu
when should together cut west window candle
que hua Bashan ye yu shi
still talk Ba-mountain night rain time[5]

You ask the date of my return: no date has been set.
The night rain over the Ba Mountains swells the
    autumn pond.
When should we together trim the candle by the
    west window,
And then talk about the time when the night rain
    fell on the Ba Mountains?
                    (Li Shangyin, "Written On a
                    Rainy Night, to be Sent North")[6]

In this poem, time is static, or at least not depicted as moving, while the speaker mentally moves forward into the future and imagines how he may feel on looking back to the present as the past. The awareness that the happy reunion envisaged for the future may in fact never take place adds to the poignancy of the present situation. Yet the poet tries to console himself and the addressee (who may or may not have been his wife) by pretending to anticipate the future with confidence, an attitude that contrasts with Christina Rossetti's gloomy skepticism in a poem that also involves the ego's moving forward into the future:

> I shall not see the shadows,
> I shall not feel the rain;
> I shall not hear the nightingale
> Sing on, as if in pain;
> And dreaming through the twilight
> That doth not rise nor set,
> Haply I may remember,
> And haply may forget.[7]

3. Ego moving forward, time moving in opposite direction:

義和驅日月
疾急不可恃
浮生雖多途
趨死惟一軌

（韓愈，秋懷詩，其一）

> *Xihe qu ri yue*
> Xihe drive sun moon
> *ji ji bu ke shi*
> fast fleet not can rely
> *fu sheng sui duo tu*
> floating life though many path
> *qu si wei yi gui*
> rush death only one track[8]

> Xihe drives the sun and moon,
> Fast, fleet, not to be relied on.
> Though this floating life has many paths,
> In rushing toward death there's only one track.
>   (Han Yu, "Autumn Meditations, No. 1")

I think that Xihe, the mythological charioteer of the sun (who seems to have temporarily taken over the duties of Wangshu, the charioteer of the moon, as well) is imagined as driving in the opposite direction from the speaker, rather than in the same direction, as Stephen Owen implies when he remarks on "this race with time,"[9] for why should anyone wish to win the race with time to reach death? If we think of the speaker as involuntarily rushing toward death while time is driving by in the opposite direction, this will reinforce the idea of speed. These lines are full of pessimism, which may be contrasted with Shakespeare's defiance of time and death:

> hear this, thou age unbred,
> Ere you were born was beauty's summer dead.[10]

Although in this sonnet the poet also sees time as moving past him, he moves forward into the future and even beyond death to proclaim his friend's supreme beauty. Paradoxically, by admitting his friend's mortality, the poet assures the latter immortality, in a subtler way than in

> Nor shall death brag thou wanderest in his shade,
> When in eternal lines to time thou growest.[11]

4. Ego moving backward (i.e., turning around and moving toward the past that was behind one), time static:

前不見古人
後不見來者
念天地之悠悠
獨愴然而涕下
（陳子昂，登幽州台歌）

qian bu jian gu ren
front not see ancient people
hou bu jian lai zhe
behind not see coming ones
nian tian di zhi youyou
think heaven earth's long-long
du chuangran er ti xia
alone sadly and tear fall[12]

In front, I do not see the ancients;
Behind, I do not see those to come.
Thinking of the vastness and long-lastingness of

> heaven and earth,
> Alone I sadly let fall my tears.
> > (Chen Zi'ang, "Song of Ascending
> > the Tower at Youzhou")

Although the use of such spatial terms as *qian* ("front" or "before") and *hou* ("behind" or "after") in relation to time is by no means simple, there are some expressions like *qiantu* ("road before," i.e., "future prospects"), *qiancheng* ("journey in front," i.e., "future career"), *qianzhan* ("look in front," i.e., "look ahead to the future"), *huigu* ("look back"), *huiyi* ("turn round and recall"), and *huixiang* ("turn back and think"), all of which suggest that the future is in front of us and the past is behind us. But in this poem Chen Zi'ang says just the opposite. I think this can be explained by saying that he is turning around and moving toward the past, so that the ancients should be in front of him and those yet to come should be behind him. His failure to see either induces a cosmic loneliness against the background of infinite time and infinite space, for the reduplicate compound *youyou* implies both spatial and temporal "length." We may compare this song with the following lines from Henry Vaughan's "The Retreat":

> O how I long to travel back,
> And tread again that ancient track!
> That I might once more reach that plain
> Where first I left my glorious train;
> From whence th'enlightened spirit sees
> That shady City of Palm-trees.
> But ah! my soul with too much stay
> Is drunk, and staggers in the way!
> Some men forward motion love,
> But I by backward steps would move;
> And when this dust falls to the urn,
> In that state I came, return.[13]

Although both poets are moving backward in time, each is typical of his own tradition: Chen Zi'ang, the good Confucian, looks nostalgically back to an idealized historical past, whereas Vaughan, the good Christian, looks nostalgically back to a presumed Heaven, as Wordsworth did later.

We can now turn to examples of Concurrence.

1. Ego static, time moving forward from behind:

故人適千里
臨別尚遲遲
人行猶可復
歲行那可追

問歲安所之
遠在天一涯
已逐東流水
赴海歸無時

（蘇軾，別歲）

gu ren shi qian li
old friend go thousand *li*
lin bie shang chichi
face parting still delay-delay
ren xing you ke fu
man travel still can return
sui xing na ke zhui
year travel how can chase
wen sui an suo zhi
ask year where that-which go
yuan zai tian yi ya
far at sky one shore
yi zhu dong liu shui
already follow east flow water
fu hai gui wu shi
go sea no return time[14]

When an old friend goes on a thousand-*li* journey,
At parting, he still lingers and delays.
A man travelling may yet return;
A year travelling: how can it be chased?
If you ask, Where is the year going?
As far as the other shore of the sky.
Already it is following the east-flowing water,
That goes to the sea, never to return.

(From Su Shi, "Farewell to the Old Year")

These lines, which form the first half of one of three poems written at the end of the year corresponding to 1062, suggest a conception of time as moving forward past the speaker. For one thing, when we say farewell to a departing friend, we see him disappear before us, not the other way. For another, the word *zhui* ("chase") also suggests that the old year is moving forward past the speaker, who is unable to chase it. This is further corroborated by the following lines from the last of the three poems:

欲知垂盡歲
有似赴壑蛇
脩鱗半已沒
去意誰能遮
況欲繫其尾
雖勤知奈何

（蘇軾，守歲）

yu zhi chui jin sui
wish know about-to end year
you si fu he she
resemble go gulley snake
xiu lin ban yi mo
long scale half already submerge
qu yi shui neng zhe
depart intent who can stop
kuang yu xi qi wei
moreover wish tie its tail
sui qin zhi naihe
though diligent know what-do[15]

You wish to know what the year about to end is like?
It's like a snake rushing into a gulley:
With half its long scaly body already submerged,
Who can stop its intention to depart,
Let alone try to tie up its tail?
No matter how hard you try, you know there's nothing
    you can do.

(From Su Shi, "Keeping Vigil on
New Year's Eve")[16]

In order to visualize this image, I think we would have to imagine the old year as a snake moving forward past the speaker and disappearing before him, rather than in the opposite direction. Su Shi's perception of time in these poems seems similar to that of Andrew Marvell:

> But at my back I always hear
> Time's wingéd chariot hurrying near;

but of course, not being a Christian, Su does not share Marvell's vision of eternity:

> And yonder all before us lie
> Deserts of vast eternity.[17]

2. Ego and time both moving forward:

壑舟無須臾
引我不得住
前塗當幾許
未知止泊處

（陶潛，雜詩，其五）

> *he zhou wu xuyu*
> gulley boat not-have moment
> *yin wo bu de zhu*
> lead me not can dwell
> *qian tu dang jixu*
> front path should how-much
> *wei zhi zhi bo chu*
> not-yet know stop moor place[18]

The boat in the gulley does not stay for a moment,
Leading me on, unable to dwell.
The path in front: how much more?
I do not yet know where I'll stop and moor.
(From Tao Qian, "Miscellaneous Poems,
No. 5")

The expression "boat in the gulley" (*he zhou*), as has been pointed out,[19] is derived from the *Zhuangzi*: "Now someone who hides a boat in a gulley . . . says that it is secure, but in the middle of the night a strong man may carry it away." However, it is used here in a different way, as an image of time. The lines just quoted are remarkably similar to Emily Dickinson's

> Down Time's quaint stream
> Without an oar
> We are enforced to sail.[20]

Nonetheless, Tao is able to adopt a more positive attitude: instead of complaining that we are forced to move forward with time, he willingly follows the flow of time:

掩淚汎東逝
順流隨時遷

（陶潛，雜詩，其九）

> *yan lei fan dong shi*
> stop tear float east depart
> *shun liu sui shi qian*
> follow flow chase time change[21]

Holding back tears, I float on that which departs eastwards;
Following its flow, I chase Time's change.
(From Tao Qian, "Miscellaneous Poems, No. 9")

It is possible that the first line refers to an actual journey east by water,[22] but we can also take it metaphorically as a reference to time. It is this attitude that enables Tao to overcome his fear of death and his sadness over human mortality:

縱浪大化中
不喜亦不懼
應盡便須盡
無復獨多慮

（陶潛，形影神）

> *zong lang dahua zhong*
> release let-go great-change midst
> *bu xi yi bu ju*
> not rejoice also not fear

ying jin bian xu jin
should end then must end
wu fu du duo lü
not again alone much care[23]

Let yourself go on the waves of Great Change,
Without joy and without fear.
When you should cease, then you must cease,
Don't be full of care alone any more.
                    (From Tao Qian, "Form, Shadow,
                    and Spirit")

In the first line, the word *lang* primarily means "let go," as part of
the compound *zong lang*, but I think it is reasonable to remember
its original meaning of "waves," as J. R. Hightower has done in his
translation of the poem,[24] and I have in the translation above. By
drifting with the flow of the Great Change, which is Time, one no
longer feels either joy or sorrow, but simply "transforms *with* things,"
which is what I think Zhuangzi meant by *wuhua*, rather than "transformation *of* things."

The examples given above illustrate how the way one perceives
time and space in relation to the self can affect one's emotional attitude to life, but, of course, no simple correlation can be established.

TEMPORAL PERSPECTIVES AND
SPATIAL IMAGES

As I have suggested elsewhere, we can discern three perspectives of
time in Chinese poetry: personal, historical, and cosmic.[25] Each may
be present by itself, or in combination with another, or with both the
other two. Of course, as soon as we speak of a "perspective" of time,
we are already employing a spatial metaphor. Furthermore, each temporal perspective tends to be correlated to certain types of spatial
imagery. For instance, the personal perspective tends to be correlated
to such images as houses, gardens, and roads; the historical perspective, to images like cities, palaces, and ruins; and the cosmic perspective, to images like mountains, rivers, and stars. We shall now see
examples of different temporal perspectives, singly or in combination,
together with their correlative spatial images, in various poems.

    1. Personal perspective:

少小離家老大回

鄉音無改鬢毛摧

兒童相見不相識

笑問客從何處來

（ 賀知章，囘鄉偶書 ）

shaoxiao li jia laoda hui
young-little leave home old-big return
xiang yin wu gai bin mao cui
native sound no change temple hair decay
ertong xiang jian bu xiang shi
children (one) see not (one) know
xiao wen ke cong he chu lai
smile ask traveller from what place come[26]

A youth, I left home; an old man, return.
My native accent unchanged, my hair over the temples
   decaying.
The children see me but do not know me;
Smiling, they ask the visitor whence he has come.
              (He Zhizhang, "Written Casually On
                   Coming Home")

The speaker of this poem is adopting a purely personal perspective
of time, contrasting his youth with his age. The pathos of the situation is brought out by a series of contrasts: between *shaoxiao* ("young-
little") and *laoda* ("old-big"), between *wu gai* ("no change") and *cui*
("decay"), between *xiang jian* ("see me"; *xiang* here does not mean
"mutual" but indicates that the verb *jian* has an object, understood to
be "me" in this case) and *bu xiang shi* ("not know me"), and between
jia ("home") and *xiang* ("native") on the one hand, and *ke* ("visitor"
or "traveller") on the other. Ironically, now that the speaker has come
home, the children in the village do not know him, and, despite his
accent, which has not changed, treat him as a stranger. Such is the
trick that time has played on him. We do not find any striking spatial
images, but the contrast between *li jia* ("leave home") and *hui* ("return") implies distance in space, as does the question *cong he chu*
("from what place"). And although the word *xiang* is used in the
sense of "native," as a modifier of *yin* ("sound"), we may recall its
primary meaning of "village" and consider it a spatial image, albeit

a submerged one.

2. Historical perspective:

Innumerable poems dubbed "poems on history" (*yongshi shi*) naturally adopt the historical perspective of time. Tao Qian, in his poem
on the knight Jing Ke (sometimes called a patriot, which is somewhat
inappropriate, since he was not a native of Yan but acted out of grati-
tude to the Prince of Yan as a *zhiji*, one who appreciated him), briefly
recounts Jing's well-known attempt to assassinate the king of Qin, and
then attributes historical consciousness to the hero:

心知去不歸
且有後世名

xin zhi qu bu gui
heart know depart not return
qie you hou shi ming
still have after age name

He knew in his heart he would never return,
But would leave his name behind forever.

As if to prove that Jing's prophecy came true, the poet concludes:

其人雖已沒
千載有餘情

（陶潛，詠荊軻）

qi ren sui yi mo
this man although already dead
qian zai you yu qing
thousand year have surplus feeling[27]

Although this man is dead and gone,
A thousand years later endless feelings remain.
(From Tao Qian, "On Jing Ke")

The last line can be taken to mean, "A thousand years later, he still
arouses endless feelings," or, "A thousand years later, *his* feelings still
remain endless."[28] However that may be, the action is seen in a historical perspective and not as an isolated event.

3. Cosmic perspective:

南風吹山作平地
帝遣天吳移海水
王母桃花千遍紅
彭祖巫咸幾回死

（李賀，浩歌）

nan feng chui shan zuo ping di
south wind blow mountain be flat ground
di qian Tianwu yi hai shui
god send monster shift sea water
Wangmu tao hua qian bian hong
Queen-mother peach blossom thousand times red
Pengzu Wuxian ji hui si
Pengzu Wuxian how-many times die[29]

The south wind blows on the mountains, turning them to
    level ground.
God sends the monster Tianwu to shift the seas.
The Queen Mother's peach flowers have reddened a thousand
    times;
How often have Pengzu and Wuxian died?
                    (From Li He, "Loud Song") [30]

These lines are truly striking for their use of cosmic spatial images
and mythological figures to convey a cosmic perspective of time. It
boggles the mind to imagine how long it would take the wind to re-
duce the mountains to level ground, the seas to shift positions, and
the peach flowers of the goddess, Queen Mother of the West, supposed
to blossom once every three thousand years, to do so a thousand times.
Against such a colossal temporal perspective, how much would several
human lifetimes amount to, even the longest ones such as those enjoyed by the legendary Pengzu and Wuxian?

4. Personal and historical perspectives combined:

搖落深知宋玉悲
風流儒雅亦吾師
帳望千秋一洒淚
蕭條異代不同時

（杜甫，詠懷古跡五首，其二）

yaoluo shen zhi Song Yu bei
shake-fall deeply know Song Yu grief
fengliu ruya yi wu shi
wind-flow scholar-elegant also my teacher
chang wang qian qiu yi sa lei
sadly gaze thousand autumn once shed tear
xiaotiao yi dai bu tong shi
lonely-desolate different age not share time[31]

"Shaking and falling": I deeply understand Song Yu's grief.
Free-spirited and elegant, he too is my mentor.
Sadly gazing toward a thousand autumns, I shed tears once;
Each lonely in a different age, we do not share the same times.
          (From Du Fu, "Thoughts on Ancient Sites, No. 2") [32]

In these lines, Du Fu first establishes a link between the personal perspective of time and the historical one by quoting partially from the
Jiubian ("Nine Arguments") attributed to Song Yu, thus identifying
with the earlier poet in spirit. Then he explicitly states that he regards
Song Yu as one of his mentors. In the third line, by saying that he is
"sadly gazing toward a thousand autumns" he spatializes time (a point
to which we shall return later), and he seems to be calling attention
to this by using a rhyming binome followed by an alliterative one
(*chang wang* followed by *qian qiu*). In this way, Du Fu comes face to
face with Song Yu, said to have lived about a thousand years earlier.
However, in the next line they become separate again, when Du Fu
painfully realizes that after all they do not live in the same age, a fact
emphasized by the use of *yi dai* ("different age") and *bu tong shi*
("not share time"). It may be noted that the last three syllables should
be taken as verb + verb + object, not as modifier + noun.

  5. Personal and cosmic perspective combined:

細草微風岸
危檣獨夜舟
星垂平野濶
月湧大江流
名豈文章著
官應老病休
飄飄何所似
天地一沙鷗

（杜甫，旅夜書懷）

xi cao wei feng an
fine grass slight wind bank
wei qiang du ye zhou
tall mast solitary night boat
xing chui ping ye kuo
star droop flat wild wide
yue yong da jiang liu
moon rush great river flow
ming qi wenzhang zhu
fame how literary-composition manifest
guan ying lao bing xiu
office should old sick retire
piaopiao he suo si
float-float what that-which resemble
tian di yi sha'ou
sky earth one sand-gull[33]

A fine-grassy, light-breezy bank,
A tall-masted solitary night boat.
Stars drooping, the flat wilds widen;
The moon bobbing, the Great River flows.
Fame: is it to be won by writings?
Office: old and sick, I should give up.
Floating, floating: what do I resemble?
Between sky and earth, a gull alone.
(Du Fu, "Writing Down My Thoughts while
    Travelling at Night") [34]

The opening couplet juxtaposes the cosmic perspective of time with
the personal, but a link between the two is established by the strategic
position of the word *du* ("solitary"): logically, it should modify the
last word of the line, *zhou* ("boat"), but syntactically, it appears to
modify the word that follows immediately, *ye* ("night"). In this way,
the solitary boat, without losing its effect as an image of the speaker's
solitude, at the same time becomes a spatial image correlated to the
night, which is a segment of time and is imagined to be as solitary as
the speaker. The second couplet adopts the cosmic perspective alone:
nature is seen as it presumably always is, not from any personal angle.
Incidentally, we may note how in each line of this couplet the poet
first presents a phenomenon and then reveals the cause: the stars ap-

pear to droop because the flat wilds are so wide, and the moon seems to bob because it is reflected in the flowing river. This inversion of cause and effect produces an element of surprise, and the use of four verbs in two lines lends a dynamic quality to the imagery. In the third couplet, the poet shifts to the personal perspective and laments his failure to achieve fame as an official. Yet, because he views his personal life against the cosmic background, he is able, in the final couplet, to release himself from his disappointments and feel as free as a sea gull floating between sky and earth, a spatial image that wonderfully combines the personal perspective with the cosmic. Some critics see nothing but despair in the last couplet,[35] but I think that the ending expresses relief rather than despair, and that the gull should be regarded as a symbol of freedom rather than solitude, for Du Fu had used the same image many years previously as a young man full of self-confidence:

白鷗沒浩蕩
萬里誰能馴
（杜甫，奉贈韋左丞丈）

bo ou mo haodang
white gull disappear vast-shake
wan li shui neng xun
myriad *li* who can tame[36]

The white gull disappears into vast waves,
For ten thousand miles: who can tame it?
(From Du Fu, "Presented to My Elder,
The Senior Secretary Wei")[37]

Here, surely, the image suggests a free spirit rather than a lonely wanderer, not to mention the fact that the gull is traditionally associated with the life of the *yinyi* (literally, "hiding and free," usually translated as "recluse," although the Chinese terms does not imply unsociable behavior but withdrawal from worldly strife and the pursuit of fame and fortune).[38]

   6. Historical and cosmic perspectives combined:

此地別燕丹
壯士髮衝冠
昔時人已沒
今日水猶寒

（駱賓王，渡易水送別）

ci di bie Yan Dan
this place part Yan Dan
zhuang shi fa chong guan
brave knight hair push hat
xishi ren yi mo
former-time man already disappear
jinri shui you han
today water still cold[39]

Here he parted from Prince Dan of Yan;
The brave knight's hair pushed up his hat.
The man of that time is dead and gone;
Today, the water of the river is still cold.
　(Luo Binwang, "Crossing River Yi to
　See Someone Off") [40]

Unlike Tao Qian, who sees the knight Jing Ke in a purely historical perspective, Luo Binwang introduces the cosmic perspective in the last line, thereby contrasting the transiency of human history with the permanency of nature.

7. Personal, historical, and cosmic perspectives combined:

牛渚西江夜
青天無片雲
登舟望秋月
空憶謝將軍
余亦能高詠
斯人不可聞
明朝掛帆去
楓葉落紛紛

（李白，夜泊牛渚懷古）

Niuzhu xi jiang ye
Ox-isle west river night
qing tian wu pian yun
blue sky no piece cloud
deng zhou wang qiu yue
climb boat gaze autumn moon
kong yi Xie jiangjun
vainly recall Xie general
yu yi neng gao yong
I too can high chant
si ren bu ke wen
this man not may hear
mingzhao gua fan qu
tomorrow-morning hang sail depart
feng ye luo fenfen
maple leaves fall disorderly-profusely[41]

Night at Ox Isle, over west river,
Clear sky, not a speck of cloud.
Climbing aboard, I gaze at the autumn moon,
Vainly recalling General Xie.
I too know how to chant loftily;
This man cannot be heard anymore.
Tomorrow morning I'll hoist my sail and depart;
The maple leaves will fall at random in profusion.
(Li Bo, "Recalling Antiquity While
Mooring at Ox Isle at Night")

The first couplet presents the cosmic perspective: there is no trace of any human being. Line 3 introduces the speaker and links the personal perspective with the cosmic by means of the word *wang* ("gaze"). Line 4 presents the historical perspective by mentioning General Xie (Xie Shang, who, as Li Bo points out in a note, heard Yuan Hong chanting his poems on history at this very spot). In line 5, the phrase *gao yong* can be taken to mean "chant aloud" or "chant on lofty themes," or both, and line 6 can be understood as "This man may not be heard anymore," or "This man cannot hear me anymore." No matter how we interpret these lines, they undoubtedly juxtapose the personal perspective with the historical. Li Bo compares himself to Yuan Hong and laments the absence of a contemporary Xie Shang to appreciate him. However, his frustration is transcended in the final couplet, in which the personal perspective submerges in the cosmic. The image of the boat sailing away into infinite space can be taken as a metaphor for the speaker's disappearing into infinite time, and the falling of the maple leaves suggests the indifference of nature to both personal and historical events. Against this cosmic perspective, one's own misfortunes appear insignificant, and the speaker transcends his sorrow.

SPATIALIZATION OF TIME AND TEMPORALIZATION OF SPACE

Apart from spatial terms commonly used to express temporal relations, such as *qian* ("before") and *hou* ("after"), we sometimes find in Chinese poetry uncommon ways of expressing temporal concepts in spatial terms and vice versa. Such expressions can be recognized by uncommon diction, imagery, or syntax. We have already seen an example of the spatialization of time in Du Fu's phrase *chang wang qian qiu*; here are a few more examples.

1.

行到水窮處
坐看雲起時

（王維，終南別業 ）

xing dao shui qiung chu
walk reach water end place
zuo kan yun qi shi
sit watch cloud rise time[42]

I walk till I reach the place where the water ends,
I sit and watch the time when the clouds rise.
(From Wang Wei, "Zhongnan Villa") [43]

This couplet involves some ambiguity. We can take *chu* ("place") and *shi* ("time") as the objects of the verbs *dao* ("reach") and *kan* ("watch") respectively, as in the translation given above, or take both lines as noun phrases instead of sentences and render them this way:

The place where I walk and reach the water's end—
The time when I sit and watch the clouds rise—

In either case, the juxtaposition of *chu* ("place") and *shi* ("time") at the end of the two lines calls attention to the interaction of space and time. In the first line, the temporal process of walking to the source of the water is spatialized by the word *chu*; in the second line, the spatial relationship between the speaker and the clouds is temporalized by the word *shi*. It may be argued that a temporal element is also present in the first line and a spatial element is also present in the second, but it is undeniable that the emphasis in the first line is on the spatial relationship between the speaker and the water's source, not on the time it takes to get there, whereas emphasis in the second line is on the temporal aspect of the experience of watching the clouds rise, not on the distance between the speaker and the clouds. Furthermore, we may note the contrasts between static and dynamic images.[44] The dynamic image *xing* ("walk") in the first line contrasts with the static *zuo* ("sit"), which occupies the corresponding position in the second line. Similarly, the static *qiung* ("end") contrasts with the dynamic *qi* ("rise"). At the same time, there is also internal contrast within each line: *xing* against *qiung* in the first line, and *zuo* against *qi* in the second. These subtle and complex imagistic contrasts, which belie the seeming simplicity of the couplet, reveal the poet's underlying perception of spatiotemporal relationships, for the static images primarily imply temporal duration, whereas the dynamic images primarily imply spatial change, although the former also involve spatial location and the latter also involve temporal process.

2.

昔人已乘黃鶴去
此地空餘黃鶴樓
黃鶴一去不復返
白雲千載空悠悠

（崔顥，黃鶴樓詩）

xi ren yi cheng huang he qu
former man already ride yellow crane depart
ci di kong yu Huang He Lou
this place empty remain Yellow Crane Tower
huang he yi qu bu fu fan
yellow crane once depart not again return

bo yun qian zai kong youyou
white cloud thousand year empty long-long[45]

The man of old has already left, riding on a yellow crane;
Here, the Yellow Crane Tower remains in vain in the
    empty air.
The yellow crane, once gone, will not return again;
The white clouds, for a thousand years, will last in vain in
    the empty air.

(From Cui Hao, "Yellow Crane Tower")

In the first couplet, although superficially *xi ren* ("former man") is contrasted with *ci di* ("this place"), the underlying contrast is really between *xi shi* ("former time") and *ci ri* ("this day"), and so it seems valid to say that the word *di* is temporalized. Alternatively, we may say that the temporal relationship between past and present is expressed in spatial terms as a contrast between "former *man*" and "this *place*." In the third line, the temporal term *yi* ("once") temporalizes the spatial image evoked by *qu* ("depart"), and the phrase *bu fu* ("not again") further temporalizes the spatial image evoked by *fan* ("return"), which already implies temporal recurrence anyway. In the next line, the temporal phrase *qian zai* ("thousand year") refers to the spatial image *bo yun* ("white cloud"), so that the reduplicative compound *youyou* ("long-long") appears to mean both "lasting long" and "extending far." At the same time, the word *kong*, which is used twice, primarily in the sense of "in vain," implies the passage of time, for it is only after a lapse of time that we realize that something has been in vain. However, we should not forget the original meaning of *kong*, "empty," and should consider "empty space" as an implication of the word. (Hence, the word-for-word translation above gives "empty" as the equivalent of *kong*.)

3.

萬里悲秋常作客
百年多病獨登台

（杜甫，登高）

wan li bei qiu chang zuo ke
myriad *li* lament autumn constantly be traveller

bo nian duo bing du deng tai
hundred year much illness alone climb tower[46]

Over a myriad miles, lamenting autumn, I am constantly
    travelling;
Within a lifespan of a hundred years, full of illness,
    I alone climb the tower.

(From Du Fu, "Climbing High")

Syntactically, the spatial *wan li* ("myriad *li*") contrasts with the temporal *bo nian* ("hundred years"), and the temporal *chang* ("constantly")
with the spatial *du* ("alone"), but semantically we may also see a contrast between *wan li* and *du*, a contrast that emphasizes the speaker's
loneliness in vast space, and one between *bo nian*, the conventional
maximum lifespan for a human being, and *chang*, a contrast that emphasizes the seeming endlessness of wandering. Thus, if we were to
transpose the first half of each of the two lines and write,

bo nian duo bing chang zuo ke
wan li bei qiu du deng tai

the couplet would still make perfect sense. The underlying interactions between time and space enrich the poetic meaning and add to
the complexity of the linguistic structure.

4.

羣山萬壑赴荆門
生長明妃尚有村
一去紫台連朔漠
獨留青塚向黃昏

（杜甫，詠懷古跡五首，其三）

qun shan wan he fu Jingmen
flock mountain myriad valley go-to Jingmen
sheng zhang Ming Fei shang you cun
bear rear Ming Fei still have village
yi qu zi tai lian shuo mo
once depart purple tower join northern desert
du liu qing zhong xiang huanghun
alone leave green tomb face yellow-dusk[47]

Amid flocks of mountains and a myriad valleys I head
for Jingmen.
Bearing and rearing Princess Ming: the village is still
there.
Once departing from the purple towers, she joined the
northern desert;
Alone she left behind the Green Tomb to face the
yellow dusk.
(From Du Fu, "Thoughts on Ancient Sites, No. 3")

These lines from Du Fu's poem on Wang Qiang, also known as Wang
Zhaojun or Ming Fei ("Bright Consort"), present some striking features. As various scholars have noticed, the syntax of the first line is
ambiguous: we can either take the implied subject to be "I," as in the
above translation and in David Hawkes's paraphrase,[48] or take *qun
shan wan he* ("flocks of mountains and myriad valleys") as the subjects, as in Hans Frankel's translation[49] and in Irving Lo's,[50] but in
either case the spatial relationship between "flocks of mountains and
myriad valleys" and the place Jingmen is rendered dynamic by the
verb *fu* ("go to"), which implies a temporal process. The syntax of
the second line is even more unusual. Instead of writing *shang you
Ming Fei sheng zhang cun*, which is what one would have expected,
Du Fu wrote, *sheng zhang Ming Fei shang you cun*, not, I believe,
simply to conform to the prescribed tone pattern or out of a desire
for novelty for its own sake, but as a daring way to spatialize time.
Had he written the former, Ming Fei would have been the subject of
sheng zhang, which then would have meant "was born and reared,"
and the clause *Ming Fei sheng zhang* would have referred to a period
in the past. As the line now stands, Ming Fei is the *object* of *sheng
zhang* ("bearing and rearing"), and the phrase *sheng zhang Ming Fei*
modifies *cun*, as if one were to say, "the bearing-and-rearing-Ming-Fei
sort of village." Thus, a past event is transformed into an attribute of
an object that still exists in space. In the next couplet, the spatial
relationship between *zi tai* ("purple tower," representing the Chinese
palace) and *shuo mo* ("northern desert") is temporalized by *yi qu*
("once gone") and *lian* ("join"), both of which involve temporal
processes; the temporal term *huanghun* ("yellow-dusk"), which denotes a specific segment of time, is spatialized by the verb *xiang*
("face"), for the yellow dusk must exist in space to be "faced" by the

tomb, which, according to legend, remains ever green in the desert. Through the spatialization of time and temporalization of space, Du Fu merges past and present, Ming Fei's native village in Sichuan and her tomb in the Mongolian desert, in the total world of the poem.

TRANSCENDENCE OF TIME AND SPACE

In some poems we see a conscious attempt to transcend time and space, such as in the following poem by Li Bo:

黃河走東溟
白日入西海
逝川與流光
飄忽不相待
春容捨我去
秋髮已衰改
人生非寒松
年貌豈長在
吾當乘雲螭
吸景駐光彩

（李白，古風五十九首，其十一）

Huanghe zou dong ming
Yellow-river run east sea
bo ri luo xi hai
white sun set west sea
shi chuan yu liu guang
vanish river and flow light
piaohu bu xiang dai
sudden-fast not (one) wait
chun rong she wo qu
spring appearance desert me depart
qiu fa yi shuai gai
autumn hair already fade change
ren sheng fei han song
human life not cold pine
nian mao qi chang zai
year visage how long exist

wu dang cheng yun chi
I should ride cloud dragon
xi jing zhu guang cai
inhale light stay bright color[51]

The Yellow River runs to the eastern ocean,
The white sun sets over the western sea.
The vanishing river and the streaming light
Both are gone suddenly, awaiting no one.
My spring looks have deserted me and gone,
My autumn hair is already fading away.
Human life is not a wintry pine:
How could years and visage remain for long?
I would ride a dragon among the clouds
To inhale celestial lights and keep my bright
   countenance.
(Li Bo, "Ancient Airs, No. 11")[52]

Both the river and the sun are, of course, common symbols of time
in Chinese poetry, but what is uncommon is the visualization of these
as moving in opposite directions in space: the Yellow River is flowing
eastward while the sun is moving westward. This emphasizes the speed
with which time passes. To transcend time and space, the poet wishes
to rise vertically, as it were, above the river and the sun's course, so
as to remain young forever.[53]

Apart from such examples of the transcendence of time and space
in individual poems, in a broader sense all poetry transcends time and
space, since, once a poem is written, it exists potentially outside time
and space, to be re-created by a reader of another time and space. As
suggested in chapter 3, all deictic expressions in a poem should be
taken as if they referred to the reader's present, or, to use Paul
Ricoeur's terminology, all "ostensive references" to an actual world
should be taken as "nonostensive references" to possible worlds.[54] By
creating a world in a linguistic structure, the poet transcends time and
space and enables countless readers to re-create the world of the poem
in their own time and space.

Epilogue

SINCE THIS BOOK is intended to be an open-ended enquiry, the interpretive process itself being conceived of as an open-ended spiral,
there can be no real conclusion. Nonetheless, it may be useful to re-
capitulate a few points made in the preceding pages, and to clarify
my position regarding certain questions that have recently been raised
by some scholars about a "common poetics." Further, I wish to discuss
briefly the relation between "interlingual criticism" and "comparative
literature," and to indicate tentative plans for future work. In this
way, the autobiographical note struck in the introduction may find an
echo toward the end.

The conceptual framework suggested in the first chapter, illustrated
(however inadequately) by the tetradic circle provides, I hope, a para-
digm by which any theory of literature or poetics can be analyzed. It
also serves as a reminder that one should keep in mind all four elements involved in a literary work of art, namely, world, author, work,
and reader. Such a reminder may be necessary in view of recent trends
toward reader-oriented theories of literature and poetics, which are
welcome reactions against earlier tendencies to regard the literary
work of art as an isolated object and to treat a literary text as if it
were fixed once for all; yet, in discussing readers' responses to a literary work of art one should not forget that the work could not have
come into being without an author and that the author could not
have existed in a vacuum but must have lived in a world, which must

have something in common with the reader's world. To read a poem is not to discover an object, but to have an intersubjective experience, and in order to have a valid intersubjective experience one needs to know something about the author's cultural world. This attitude does not lead to positive historicism or total historical relativism, but to an awareness of both the author's and the reader's own historicity, an awareness that should, paradoxically, enable one to transcend historical and cultural barriers and to plunge imaginatively into another world. That is all I mean by "transhistoricism" and "transculturism": not the attainment of some universal and transcendent realm above all historical periods and human cultures, but the crossing of boundaries, just as "Trans World Airlines" does not transport us to some supraterrestrial sphere but simply allows us to cross geographical and political boundaries.

The above remarks betray my sympathy with Etièmble, who has been criticized for his belief in "invariables littéraires" by D. W. Fokkema in the latter's article "New Strategies in the Comparative Study of Literature and Their Application to Contemporary Chinese Literature."[1] Even though certain artistic elements in a literary work may not be received as such by certain readers in a given society at a given moment in history, this should not prevent *us* from attempting to identify them and see if they are to be found in works belonging to more than one age, or culture, or society. A search for such artistic elements and aesthetic effects could lead to a genuinely comparative poetics, if not a common poetics.

A. Owen Aldridge, both in his article "East-West Relations: Universal Literature, Yes; Common Poetics, No"[2] and in his introduction to the volume *China and the West: Comparative Literature Studies*,[3] offers some sobering thoughts on the indiscriminate application of modern Western critical methods to Chinese literature, and argues against the possibility of a common poetics by pointing out that Western criticism is not monolithic. Likewise, André Lefevere deplores the current situation in Western criticism: "What we witness is not the development of a scientific discipline, but a battle between conflicting ideologies."[4] With these sentiments I heartily agree, and when I speak of a "synthesis of Chinese and Western theories of literature," of course I do not mean a grand synthesis of *all* Chinese and Western theories, but only one of *some* elements of certain Chinese theories and *some* elements of certain Western ones.

The reason why I advocate synthesis rather than pluralism or eclecticism, as does Aldridge, who believes that "it is possible both to consider critical pluralism superior to dogmatic absolutism and to admit the value of eclecticism, both as an abstract principle and as a critical approach,"[5] is that I believe that consistency is one of the five cardinal virtues to which a critic should aspire (the other four being breadth, depth, rigor, and originality). One cannot, for instance, be a structuralist one moment and a phenomenologist the next. As far as an individual critic's work is concerned, synthesis is not only desirable but necessary. Even where all critics are concerned, pluralism should not be equated with the abandonment of all standards and the misguided application of the principle of democracy to intellectual endeavors, to the effect that all theories of literature and all critical approaches are created equal. Some current Western critical methods are of dubious value when applied to Chinese literature and contain an inherent danger of not seeing the tree for the woods, or in other words, of not seeing the unique qualities of a literary work of art but only seeing the common thematic, generic, or structural features it shares with other works in the same language or in other languages. My wish to search for artistic and aesthetic qualities that transcend linguistic, cultural, and historical barriers has not blinded me to this danger.

Next, I should like to clarify what I believe to be the relation between "interlingual criticism" and "comparative literature." When I wrote, "The application of modern Western approaches to Chinese literature implicitly involves a comparative dimension,"[6] I did so not to defend such applications as a legitimate branch of comparative literature, as Aldridge thought, but rather to hint at the fact that as soon as one uses such Western terms as "metaphor," "motif," "genre," or even "poetry," one is implicitly comparing Chinese literature with Western literature and raising the question whether these terms have the same meanings when applied to Chinese works. Thus, anyone who writes in one language about literature that it is written in another language is perforce a comparativist to some extent. Indeed, one might say that some are born comparativists, some achieve comparativity, and some have comparativity thrust upon them. As an inter-

lingual critic, I am less concerned about the question whether interlingual criticism should be accepted as part of comparative literature
than the question whether comparativists should pay more attention
to problems of interlingual criticism, instead of assuming that one can
discuss literature without taking into due consideration the language
in which the work concerned is written and the language in which
oneself is writing. I can see no way for anyone writing in English about
Chinese literature to avoid asking comparative questions. Even the
use of the word "literature" itself begs the question: is what we call
"literature" in English the same as what is called *wen* in Chinese?
The question cannot be solved, as some critics think, by saying that
"literature" is simply what a community decides to treat as such, for
the question immediately arises as to who constitutes the community
that decides what literature is. In dealing with traditional Chinese
writings, are we talking about the community of the author's own
time, or contemporary Chinese readers, or contemporary Western
readers? Even in a single society, such as the contemporary society in
the U.S.A., how should we define the literary community: the literary
establishment of the East Coast, or professors of literature, or the editors and readers of such popular magazines as *Time* and *Reader's
Digest*, all of whom have rather different notions as to what "literature" is? Every interlingual critic has to try to answer the question
for himself.

I should further emphasize that when I mentioned the "tacit
assumptions that comparable features and qualities exist between
Chinese and Western literatures and that comparable standards are
applicable to both,"[7] I certainly did not intend to endorse such assumptions but to question them. In fact, the present book is largely
a result of this questioning. On the other hand, inveterate optimist
that I am, I still think it possible to explore common areas between
Chinese and Western poetry and poetics.

One such area that I am currently interested in is the poetics of
paradox, by which I do not mean Cleanth Brooks's well-known theory
that the language of paradox is the language of poetry, but rather the
poetics based on the paradox of language: it is the indispensable medium of artistic expression for the poet, yet poets for centuries, both
in China and in the West, have complained that ultimate reality

cannot be fully expressed in language. This paradox of language is further compounded by the paradox of art, which is both more real and less real than reality. And when it comes to literary criticism, yet another paradox is involved: the literary critic, unlike the music critic or art critic, has to use the same medium, language, as the artist whom he dares to criticize, thus suffering from the same limitations of the medium itself, as the poet and critic Lu Ji realized over sixteen centuries ago. However, I must not anticipate my next book.

NOTES

Introduction

1. See James J. Y. Liu, *Chinese Theories of Literature* (Chicago: The University of Chicago Press, 1975).

2. George Steiner, *Language and Silence* (New York: Atheneum, 1967), p. 9.

3. James J. Y. Liu, *Elizabethan and Yuan* (London: China Society Occasional Papers No. 8, 1955).

4. James J. Y. Liu, *The Art of Chinese Poetry* (Chicago: The University of Chicago Press, 1962).

5. James J. Y. Liu, "Towards a Chinese Theory of Poetry," *Yearbook of Comparative and General Literature*, No. 15 (1966). Reprinted with slight revisions in *The Poetry of Li Shang-yin* (Chicago: The University of Chicago Press, 1969).

6. Liu, *The Art of Chinese Poetry*, p. 96.

7. Liu, *The Poetry of Li Shang-yin*, p. 202.

8. Ibid.

9. Mikel Dufrenne, *Le Poétique* (Paris: Presses Universitaires de France, 1963), p. 6; *Language and Philosophy*, trans. H. B. Veatch (Bloomington: Indiana University Press, 1963), p. 80; *Phénoménologie de l'expérience esthétique* (2d ed., Paris: Presses Universitaires de France, 1967), p. 679; English translation as *The Phenomenology of Aesthetic Experience* by Edward S. Casey et al. (Evanston: Northwestern University Press, 1973), p. 554.

10. Roman Ingarden, *The Literary Work of Art*, trans. George G. Grabowicz (Evanston: Northwestern University Press, 1973), p. 357. Similar ideas have been expressed by others, e.g., Georges Poulet, "Phenomenology of Reading," *New Literary History*, Vol. I, No. 1 (1969), pp. 53–68.

11. Liu, *The Poetry of Li Shang-yin*, p. 202.

12. Ingarden, *The Literary Work of Art*, pp. lxxix–lxxxiii.

13. For further discussions, see A. C. Graham, " 'Being' in Classical Chinese," in John W. M. Verhaar, ed., *The Verb 'Be' and Its Synonyms* (Dordrecht: D. Reidel, 1967).

14. *Journal of Chinese Philosophy*, Vol. 4 (1977).

Chapter 1. The Tetradic Circle

1. This diagram is a modified version of the one I used in *Chinese Theories of Literature*. D. W. Fokkema, in his review of this book in *Dutch Quarterly Review of Anglo-American Letters*, Vol. 8 (1978), and in his article "Chinese and Renaissance Artes Poeticae," *Comparative Literature Studies*, Vol. XV, No. 2 (1978), questioned why I adopted M. H. Abrams's model for the analysis of theories of literature rather than Roman Jakobson's as developed in his well-known "Linguistics and Poetics," in Thomas A. Sebeok, ed., *Style in Language* (Cambridge, Mass.: MIT Press, 1960). Actually, since I have rearranged the four elements in a circular diagram instead of Abrams's triangular one, I am not really following his model. As for Jakobson's, for one thing I think the terms "message" and "code" tend to revive the old dichotomy between "content" and "form," and there are other questionable points such as those raised by Mary Louise Pratt in her book, *Toward a Speech Act Theory of Literary Discourse* (Bloomington: Indiana University Press, 1977).

2. For the theory that literature is imitation speech act, see Richard Ohmann, "Speech Acts and the Definition of Literature," *Philosophy and Rhetoric*, Vol. 4 (1971); and his "Literature as Act" in Seymour Chatman, ed., *Approaches to Poetics* (New York and London: Columbia University Press, 1973). For arguments against Ohmann's use of fictionality as criterion for literature, see Pratt, *Toward a Speech Act Theory of Literary Discourse*, pp. 91–96.

3. The *locus classicus* of "locutionary, illocutionary, and perlocutionary acts" is J. L. Austin's *How To Do Things with Words* (New York: Oxford University Press, 1962). Austin's theory has been elaborated by others, e.g., John R. Searle, *Speech Acts: An Essay in the Philosophy of Language* (London: Cambridge University Press, 1969); Samuel Levin, "Concerning What Kind of Speech Act a Poem Is," in T. A. Van Dijk, ed., *Pragmatics of Language and Literature* (Amsterdam: North-Holland Publishing Co., 1976).

4. *Wang Youcheng ji zhu, juan* 7, 6b.

5. See Stanley E. Fish, "How Ordinary is Ordinary Language?" *New Literary History*, Vol. V, No. 1 (1973); John M. Ellis, *The Theory of Literary Criticism* (Berkeley, Los Angeles, and London: University of California Press, 1974), p. 27; and Pratt, *Toward a Speech Act Theory of Literary Discourse*, pp. 3–37.

6. Tzvetan Todorov in his article "The Notion of Literature," *New Literary History*, Vol. V, No. 1 (1973), concludes by saying, "perhaps literature does not exist?" (p. 16).

7. See William P. Alston, *Philosophy of Language* (Englewood Cliffs, N.J.: Prentice-Hall, 1964), pp. 88–95.

8. For "occasion," see Søren Kierkegaard, *Either/Or*, trans. D. F. and L. M. Swanson (London: Oxford University Press, 1946), I, pp. 193–95.

9. *Renjian cihua*, with notes by Xu Tiaofu (Peking, 1955), p. 3.

10. Liu, *The Art of Chinese Poetry*, p. 99.

11. M. H. Abrams, *The Mirror and the Lamp* (New York: Oxford University Press, 1958), pp. 272–85.

12. R. G. Collingwood, *The Principles of Art* (Oxford: Clarendon Press, 1938), pp. 128–30.

13. Ibid.

14. Ingarden, *The Literary Work of Art*, p. 243.

15. Ibid., p. 218. Original italics.

16. Ibid., p. 221. Original italics.

17. Jean-Paul Sartre, *The Psychology of Imagination* (New York: Philosophical Library, 1948), p. 278.

18. Mikel Dufrenne, *Phénoménologie de l'expérience esthétique*, p. 244; English translation, p. 186.

19. Ibid., p. 235; English translation, p. 178.

20. Jiang Kui, *Baishi shishuo* (*Lidai shihua* ed.), p. 1.

21. Yan Yu, *Canglang shihua* (*Lidai shihua* ed.), pp. 3, 18, 19.

22. Wang Guowei, *Renjian cihua*, pp. 5, 18, 19.

23. Dufrenne, *Phénoménologie de l'expérience esthétique*, p. 235; English translation, p. 177.

24. *Baishi shishuo*, p. 4; quoted in Liu, *Chinese Theories of Literature*, p. 45.

25. Liu, *Chinese Theories of Literature*, pp. 43–45.

26. Jacques Maritain, *Creative Intuition in Art and Poetry* (New York: Pantheon Books, 1953), pp. 141–45.

27. Lu Ji, *Wenfu*, in *Lu Shiheng ji* (*Sibu beiyao* ed.), p. 2; quoted in Liu, *Chinese Theories of Literature*, pp. 72–73.

28. Li He, *Li Changji geshi* (Shanghai: Zhonghua shuju, 1958), p. 154.

29. Xie He, *Siming shihua* (*Lidai shihua* ed.), *juan* 3, p. 2; quoted in *Chinese Theories of Literature*, pp. 40–41.

30. Ye Xie, *Yuan shi* (*Qing shihua* ed.), p. 2.

31. John Dewey, *Art as Experience* (New York: Minton, Balch & Co., 1934), p. 54.

32. Paul Ricoeur, "The Model of the Text," *New Literary History*, Vol. V, No. 1 (1973), p. 96. See also his *The Conflict of Interpretations* (Evanston: Northwestern University Press, 1974).

33. E. D. Hirsch, Jr., *Validity in Interpretation* (New Haven: Yale University Press, 1967), pp. 7–9.

34. James J. Y. Liu, *Major Lyricists of the Northern Sung* (Princeton: Princeton University Press, 1974), p. 6.

35. W. K. Wimsatt, Jr., *The Verbal Icon* (Lexington: University of Kentucky Press, 1967), pp. 69–83.

36. *Western Humanities Review*, March 1970, p. 355.

37. Northrop Frye, *Anatomy of Criticism* (New York: Atheneum, 1970), pp. 73–82.

Chapter 2. The Critic as Reader

1. John M. Ellis, *The Theory of Literary Criticism*, pp. 20–22.

2. Wolfgang Iser, "The Reading Process: a Phenomenological Approach," *New Literary History*, Vol. III, No. 2 (1972), reprinted in his *The Implied*

Reader (Baltimore and London: Johns Hopkins University Press, 1974). For further discussions, see his *The Act of Reading* (Baltimore and London: Johns Hopkins University Press, 1978).

3. Edmund Husserl, *Logical Investigations*, trans. N. Findlay (New York: Humanities Press, 1970), pp. 314–15, quoted in Robert Magliola, *Phenomenology and Literature* (W. Lafayette, Indiana: Purdue University Press, 1977), p. 103.

4. Ibid. Paul Ricoeur echoes Husserl on this point in his *Interpretation Theory* (Fort Worth: Texas Christian University Press, 1976), p. 13.

5. *Yuxisheng shi jianzhu (Sibu beiyao* ed.), *juan* 2, 35a.

6. Translation adapted from Liu, *The Poetry of Li Shang-yin*, p. 152.

7. Ibid.

8. *A Concordance to the Poems of Tu Fu*, Harvard-Yenching Sinological Index Series, Supplement 14, p. 54.

9. Translation reprinted with slight revisions from James J. Y. Liu, *Essentials of Chinese Literary Art* (North Scituate, Mass.: Duxbury Press, 1979), pp. 20–21.

10. *Li Taibo shiji (Sibu beiyao* ed.), *juan* 6, 12b. Translation published for the first time.

11. Cf. Bernhard Karlgren, *The Book of Odes* (Stockholm: Museum of Far Eastern Antiquities, 1974), No. 94. For the interpretation of the last word, *zang*, as "hide," see Qu Wanli, *Shijing shiyi* (Taibei, 1953), p. 63.

12. Translation reprinted from Liu, *Essentials of Chinese Literary Art*, p. 16.

13. Ingarden, *The Literary Work of Art*, pp. 246, 250, 280, 331, 338, 341.

14. *A Concordance to the Poems of Tu Fu*, p. 80.

15. It should be noted that *jimo* here means "unheard of" or "obscure" and modifies *shen* ("person" or "life"), not *shi* ("affair"). Despite William Hung's correct paraphrase of the last line as "Will rise after an unappreciated life is past" in his *Tu Fu: China's Greatest Poet* (Cambridge, Mass.: Harvard University Press, 1952), p. 134, subsequent translators have persisted in rendering *jimo* as "forlorn," "lonely," or "paltry," and regarding it as modifying *shi*. There is no reason why Du Fu should think of posthumous fame this way; he is lamenting the lack of fame during his lifetime. See David Hawkes, *A Little Primer of Tu Fu* (Oxford: Clarendon Press, 1967), p. 97; A. R. Davis, *Tu Fu* (New York: Twayne, 1971), p. 148; Eugene Eoyang's translation in Wu-chi Liu and Irving Yucheng Lo, eds., *Sunflower Splendor* (New York: Anchor Press/Doubleday, 1975), p. 129; Wai-lim Yip, *Chinese Poetry: Major Modes and Genres* (Berkeley, Los Angeles and London: University of California Press, 1976), p. 392. In fact, Du Fu's use of *jimo* here is similar to Li Bo's in the line *gulai shengxian jie jimo (Li Taibo shiji, juan* 3, 13b)— erroneously translated by Arthur Waley as "The Saints and Sages of old times are all stock and still" in his *The Poetry and Career of Li Po* (London: Allen and Unwin, 1950), p. 46, but correctly though freely rendered by A. C. Graham as "They lie forgotten, the sages of old," in Cyril Birch, ed., *An Anthology of Chinese Literature*, Vol. I (New York: Grove Press, 1965), p. 232. Li Bo is also using *jimo* in the sense of "unheard of," in ironic contrast to the next line, *wei you yinzhe liu qi ming*, "Only drinkers have left their names behind."

16. See Liu, *The Poetry of Li Shang-yin*, pp. 138–43.

17. Shuen-fu Lin, *The Transformation of the Chinese Lyrical Tradition: Chiang K'uei and Southern Sung Tz'u Poetry* (Princeton: Princeton University Press, 1976), pp. 65–93.

18. Yu Shouzhen, *Tang shi sanbaishou xiangxi* (Hong Kong: Zhonghua shuju, 1959), p. 282. Translation published for the first time.

19. E. D. Hirsch, Jr., *Validity in Interpretation*, pp. 78 ff.

20. For an example, see J. R. Hightower, "The *Wen Hsüan* and Genre Theory," *Harvard Journal of Asiatic Studies*, Vol. 20, Nos. 3–4 (1957).

21. Benedetto Croce, *Aesthetic as Science of Expression and General Linguistic*, trans. Douglas Ainslie (London: Macmillan & Co., 1929), p. 38.

22. See Liu, *Major Lyricists of the Northern Sung*, pp. 121 ff.

23. For the *yuefu*, see Hans H. Frankel, "Yüeh-fu Poetry," in Cyril Birch, ed., *Studies in Chinese Literary Genres* (Berkeley, Los Angeles and London: University of California Press, 1974), pp. 69–101.

24. Hong Shunlong, *Xie Xuancheng ji jiaozhu* (Taibei, 1969), p. 194. New translation.

25. Ibid.

26. E.g., in the *Tang shi sanbaishou*.

27. *Li Taibo shiji, juan* 5, 12a. New translation.

Chapter 3. The Critic as Translator

1. Jan W. Walls has made a similar distinction between "poet-translator" and "pedagogical-literary translator" in his article "The Craft of Translating Poetic Structures and Patterns: Fidelity to Form," *Yearbook of Comparative and General Literature*, No. 24 (1975).

2. James J. Y. Liu, "Polarity of Aims and Methods: Naturalization or Barbarization?" ibid.

3. Quoted with approval by Achilles Fang in "Some Reflections on the Difficulty of Translation," in Reuben A. Brower, ed., *On Translation* (Cambridge, Mass.: Harvard University Press, 1959), p. 133.

4. Quoted in Paul Selver, *The Art of Translating Poetry* (Boston: The Writer, Inc., 1966), p. 26.

5. Walter Benjamin, *Illuminations*, ed. with an introduction by Hannah Arendt, trans. Harry Zohn (New York: Harcourt, Brace, and World, 1968), pp. 80–81.

6. Arthur Cooper, *Li Po and Tu Fu* (Harmondsworth, Middlesex, England: Penguin Books, 1971), p. 49.

7. Review of Burton Watson's *Chinese Rhyme-prose*, in *Asia Major*, Vol. XVIII, Pt. 2 (1973), p. 253.

8. See Wai-lim Yip, *Chinese Poetry: Major Modes and Genres*, Introduction.

9. Liu, *The Art of Chinese Poetry*, pp. 40–41.

10. This line occurs in two anonymous ancient poems.

11. Wu-chi Liu and Irving Yucheng Lo, eds., *Sunflower Splendor*, p. 131.

12. *Wang Youcheng ji zhu, juan* 7, 11b.

13. For a somewhat fuller discussion, see Liu, *Essentials of Chinese Literary Art*, pp. 26–27.

14. Elizabeth Closs Traugott, "On the Expression of Spatiotemporal Relations in Language," in Joseph H. Greenberg, Charles A. Ferguson, and Edith A. Moravcsik, eds., *Universals of Human Language*, Vol. 3 (Stanford: Stanford University Press, 1978).

15. *Li Taibo shiji, juan 23*, 10a. New translation.

16. Burton Watson, *Chinese Lyricism* (New York: Columbia University Press, 1971), p. 7.

17. *Wang Youcheng ji zhu, juan 13*, 2a.

18. *The Art of Chinese Poetry*, p. 40.

19. Shakespeare, *Macbeth*, I, vii, 25–28.

20. Shakespeare, *Romeo and Juliet*, II, i, 15–18.

21. Roman Ingarden, *The Cognition of the Literary Work of Art*, trans. Ruth Ann Crowley and Kenneth R. Olson (Evanston: Northwestern University Press, 1973), pp. 50–52.

22. A notable exception is Eugene Eoyang, who emphasized the importance of "tone" in his article "The Tone of the Poet and the Tone of the Translator," *Yearbook of Comparative and General Literature*, No. 24 (1975).

Chapter 4. The Critic as Interpreter

1. Peter Szondi, "Introduction to Literary Hermeneutics," *New Literary History*, Vol. X, No. 1 (1978), pp. 17–28.

2. D. W. Fokkema, "Cultural Relativism and Comparative Literature," *Tamkang Review*, Vol. III, No. 2 (1972), p. 60.

3. Quoted in Wellek, *Concepts of Criticism* (New Haven: Yale University Press, 1963), p. 12.

4. Ibid.

5. For a somewhat different definition of historicism, see Fokkema, "Cultural Relativism and Comparative Literature," p. 59.

6. Wellek, *Concepts of Criticism*, p. 7.

7. Roy Harvey Pearce, *Historicism Again* (Princeton: Princeton University Press, 1969), p. 19.

8. For the terms "presentism" and "presenticentrism," see Fokkema, "Cultural Relativism and Comparative Literature," p. 60.

9. J. D. Frodsham, *New Perspectives in Chinese Literature* (Canberra: Australian National University Press, 1970).

10. E. D. Hirsch, Jr., *The Aims of Interpretation* (Chicago: The University of Chicago Press, 1976), p. 4.

11. René Wellek and Austin Warren, *Theory of Literature*, 3d ed. (New York: Harcourt, Brace and World, 1962), p. 43. This use of the term "perspectivism" differs from Hirsch's, which refers to psychological and historical skepticism. See *The Aims of Interpretation*, p. 27.

12. Wellek, *Concepts of Criticism*, pp. 16–17.

13. Fokkema, "Cultural Relativism and Comparative Literature," p. 63.

14. Wellek, *Concepts of Criticism*, p. 19.

15. Ricoeur, *Interpretation Theory*, ch. 2.

16. As every linguist knows, though perhaps not every Sinologist, the distinction between *langue* and *parole* was first made by Ferdinand de Saussure.

17. Hans Robert Jauss, "The Alterity and Modernity of Medieval Litera-

ture," *New Literary History*, Vol. X, No. 2 (1979), p. 182.

18. Hirsch, *Validity in Interpretation*, p. 8.

19. Hirsch, *The Aims of Interpretation*, p. 19.

20. *Yuxisheng shi jianzhu, juan* 6, 31b.

21. Liu, *The Poetry of Li Shang-yin*, p. 160.

22. It is interesting that the anonymous compilers of *Li Shangyin shixuan* ("Selected Poems of Li Shangyin," Peking, 1978) also prefer a more general interpretation to an allegorical one (p. 206).

23. Ricoeur, *Interpretation Theory*, p. 74.

24. Hirsch, *The Aims of Interpretation*, p. 32. John M. Ellis describes a similar process, which he calls "interpretative cycle," in *The Theory of Literary Criticism*, pp. 194–210.

25. *A Concordance to the Poems of Tu Fu*, p. 63. For an unpunctuated text, see the *Sibu beiyao* edition, *juan* 2, 1a-b.

26. Qiu Zhao'ao, *Du shi xiangzhu, juan* 4, 24a.

Chapter 5. The Critic as Arbiter

1. Fokkema, "Cultural Relativism and Comparative Literature," p. 65.

2. Wellek, *Concepts of Criticism*, p. 17.

3. Ingarden, "Artistic and Aesthetic Values," in Harold Osborne, ed., *Aesthetics* (London: Oxford University Press, 1972), p. 46.

4. Ibid., pp. 48–52.

5. Dufrenne, *Phenomenology of Aesthetic Experience*, pp. 61–63.

6. Ibid., p. 62.

7. Collingwood, *The Principles of Art*, pp. 109–11.

8. T. S. Eliot, *Notes Towards the Definition of Culture* (New York: Harcourt, Brace, 1949), p. 118.

9. Liu, *The Poetry of Li Shang-yin*, p. 205.

10. *A Concordance to the Poems of Tu Fu*, p. 409.

11. Han Yu, *Han Changli quanji* (*Sibu beiyao* ed.), *juan* 16, 11a.

12. Zhao Yi, *Oubei shihua* (Peking: Renmin wenxue chubanshe, 1963), pp. 19, 31, 32, 38, 39, 63, 184–86.

13. Liu, *Chinese Theories of Literature*, pp. 36–37, 90–92.

14. Ibid., pp. 79–81.

15. The second character in Li Bi's name is usually given as 璧 , with the "jade" radical beneath, but according to the *Siku quanshu zongmu, juan* 153, 44a, it should be written 壁 , with the "earth" radical.

16. Wang Anshi, *Linchuan xiansheng wenji* (Shanghai: Zhonghua shuju, 1958), p. 310. I published a slightly different translation of this poem in *Renditions*, No. 1 (Hong Kong, 1973).

17. Qian Zhongshu, ed., *Song shi xuanzhu* (Peking: Renmin wenxue chubanshe, 1958), pp. 25–26.

18. Ibid.

19. *Wang Youcheng ji zhu, juan* 13, 7b. New translation.

20. The title of Monk Xianzhong's poem is partially homophonous with Wang Wei's, though not written with identical characters.

21. Abrams, *The Mirror and the Lamp*, pp. 71–72.

22. See note 6 to chapter 2.

23. Victor Erlich, "Limits of the Biographical Approach," *Comparative Literature*, Vol. VI (1954), p. 133.

24. See Liu, *Major Lyricists of the Northern Sung*, pp. 48–49; *Essentials of Chinese Literary Art*, pp. 18–19.

25. Hirsch, *The Aims of Interpretation*, pp. 124–45.

26. George Steiner, "Critic/Reader," *New Literary History*, Vol. X, No. 3 (1979), pp. 436 ff.

Chapter 6. A Critical Exercise

1. Elizabeth Closs Traugott, "On the Expression of Spatiotemporal Relations in Language," in Joseph H. Greenberg, Charles A. Ferguson, and Edith A. Moravcsik, eds., *Universals of Human Language*, Vol. 3 (Stanford: Stanford University Press, 1978).

2. *Li Taibo shiji, juan* 18, 13b. Also in Yu Shouzhen, *Tang shi sanbaishou xiangxi*, p. 66.

3. Shakespeare, *Macbeth*, V, v, 19–20.

4. Guillaume Apollinaire, "Le Pont Mirabeau," in *Alcools* (Paris: Éditions de la Nouvelle Revue Française, 1920), p. 16.

5. *Yuxisheng shi jianzhu, juan* 3, 30b.

6. Reprinted with slight revisions from Liu, *The Poetry of Li Shang-yin*, p. 150.

7. Christina Georgina Rossetti, "Song," in Sir Arthur Quiller-Couch, ed., *The Oxford Book of English Verse* (Oxford: Clarendon Press, 1939), pp. 964–65.

8. *Han Changli quanji, juan* 1, 22b.

9. Stephen Owen, *The Poetry of Meng Chiao and Han Yü* (New Haven and London: Yale University Press, 1975), p. 258.

10. Shakespeare, Sonnet CIV.

11. Shakespeare, Sonnet XVIII.

12. In Yu Shouzhen, *Tang shi sanbaishou xiangxi*, p. 54. New translation.

13. Henry Vaughan, "The Retreat," in *The Oxford Book of English Verse*, p. 407.

14. *Dongpo ji* (*Sibu beiyao* ed.), *juan* 1, 4b. New translation.

15. Ibid. New translation.

16. Cf. Burton Watson, trans., *Su Tung-p'o: Selections from a Sung Dynasty Poet* (New York and London: Columbia University Press, 1965), p. 26.

17. Andrew Marvell, "To His Coy Mistress," in *The Oxford Book of English Verse*, p. 399.

18. *Jingjie xiansheng ji* (*Sibu beiyao* ed.), *juan* 4, 5b. New translation.

19. J. R. Hightower, trans., *The Poetry of T'ao Ch'ien* (Oxford: Clarendon Press, 1970), p. 191.

20. *The Poems of Emily Dickinson*, ed. Thomas H. Johnson (Cambridge, Mass.: The Belknap Press of Harvard University Press, 1955), Vol. III, p. 1131 (No. 1656).

21. *Jingjie xiansheng ji, juan* 4, 6b. New translation.

22. Hightower, *The Poetry of T'ao Ch'ien*, p. 198.

23. *Jingjie xiansheng ji, juan* 2, 2a-b. New translation.

24. Hightower, *The Poetry of T'ao Ch'ien*, p. 44.

25. Liu, *Major Lyricists of the Northern Sung*, p. 155.

26. Yu Shouzhen, *Tang shi sanbaishou xiangxi*, p. 290. New translation.

27. *Jingjie xiansheng ji, juan* 4, 12a.

28. Cf. Hightower, *The Poetry of T'ao Ch'ien*, p. 224, and James J. Y. Liu, *The Chinese Knight-Errant* (Chicago: The University of Chicago Press, 1967), p. 78.

29. *Li Changji geshi*, p. 54. New translation.

30. Cf. A. C. Graham, trans., *Poems of the Late T'ang* (Harmondsworth, Middlesex, England: Penguin Books, 1965), p. 100.

31. *A Concordance to the Poems of Tu Fu*, p. 472. New translation.

32. Cf. Hans Frankel, *The Flowering Plum and the Palace Lady* (New Haven and London: Yale University Press, 1976), p. 117.

33. *A Concordance to the Poems of Tu Fu*, p. 415. I have adopted the variant reading 應 for 因 in line 6 and 飄飄 for 飄零 in line 8.

34. This version differs somewhat from the one I made jointly with Irving Lo in *Sunflower Splendor*, p. 143.

35. David Hawkes, *A Little Primer of Tu Fu*, p. 202.

36. *A Concordance to the Poems of Tu Fu*, p. 1.

37. Cf. William Hung, *Tu Fu: China's Greatest Poet*, pp. 56–57.

38. For a perceptive discussion of this poem in a different context and from a different point of view, see Shuen-fu Lin, *The Transformation of the Chinese Lyrical Tradition*, pp. 100–106.

39. *Luo Cheng Ji (Congshu jicheng* ed.), *juan* 4, 73.

40. Reprinted with slight revisions from Liu, *The Chinese Knight-Errant*, p. 79.

41. *Li Taibo shiji, juan* 22, 20b. Also in Yu Shouzhen, *Tang shi sanbaishou xiangxi*, p. 170. New translation.

42. *Wang Youcheng ji zhu, juan* 3, 4b. Also in Yu Shouzhen, *Tang shi sanbaishou xiangxi*, p. 150.

43. Cf. Wai-lim Yip, *Chinese Poetry: Major Modes and Genres*, p. 252, where the translation omits the words for *chu* and *shi*.

44. I am using the terms "dynamic image" and "static image" with regard to semantics only, irrespective of whether a word is a noun or a verb. In this I differ from Kao Yu-kung and Mei Tsu-lin, who appear to identify the former with verb and the latter with noun. See their article, "Syntax, Diction, and Imagery in T'ang Poetry," *Harvard Journal of Asiatic Studies*, Vol. 31 (1971).

45. Yu Shouzhen, *Tang shi sanbaishou xiangxi*, p. 214. New translation.

46. *A Concordance to the Poems of Tu Fu*, p. 411.

47. Ibid., p. 472. New translation.

48. Hawkes, *A Little Primer of Tu Fu*, p. 177.

49. Frankel, *The Flowering Plum and the Palace Lady*, p. 117.

50. *Sunflower Splendor*, p. 140.

51. *Li Taibo shiji, juan* 2, 9a.

52. I published a different translation of this poem in *Oriental Art*, Vol. III, No. 4 (Oxford, 1951).

53. I owe the idea for this interpretation to a former student of mine, Dr. Cynthia Chennault.

54. Paul Ricoeur, "The Model of the Text," *New Literary History*, Vol. V, No. 1 (1973), p. 96.

Epilogue

1. In William Tay, Ying-hsiung Chou, and Heh-hsiang Yuan, eds., *China and the West: Comparative Literature Studies* (Hong Kong: The Chinese University Press, 1980).

2. In *Tamkang Review*, Vol. X, Nos. 1 and 2 (1979).

3. See note 1 above.

4. Ibid., p. 13.

5. Ibid., p. iii.

6. "The Study of Chinese Literature in the West: Recent Developments, Current Trends, Future Prospects," *Journal of Asian Studies*, Vol. XXXV, No. 1 (1975), p. 28.

7. Ibid.

BIBLIOGRAPHY

(This bibliography consists only of works cited
or mentioned in the text or in the notes.)

A. Works in Chinese

Du Fu 杜甫. *A Concordance to the Poems of Tu Fu* 杜詩引得 . Harvard-
Yenching Sinological Index Series, Supplement 14.

————. *Du Gongbu shiji* 杜工部詩集 (*Sibu beiyao* 四部備要).

————. *Du shi xiangzhu* 杜詩詳註 . Edited by Qiu Zhao'ao 仇兆鰲 .

Han Yu 韓愈 . *Han Changli quanji* 韓昌黎全集 (*Sibu beiyao*).

Ji Yun 紀昀 et al., eds. *Siku quanshu zongmu* 四庫全書總目 . Taibei: Yiwen
yinshuguan 藝文印書館 .

Jiang Kui 姜夔 . *Baishi shishuo* 白石詩說 . In He Wenhuan, ed., *Lidai
shihua* 何文煥 , 歷代詩話 .

Li Bo (Li Bai) 李白 . *Li Taibo shiji* 李太白詩集 (*Sibu beiyao*).

Li He 李賀 . *Li Changji geshi* 李長吉歌詩 . Edited by Wang Chi 王琦 et
al. Shanghai: Zhonghua shuju 中華書局 , 1959.

Li Shangyin 李商隱 . *Yuxisheng shi jianzhu* 玉溪生詩箋注 . Edited by Feng
Hao 馮浩 (*Sibu beiyao*).

————. *Li shangyin shi xuan* 李商隱詩選 .   Edited by Anhui Shida
Zhong-wenxi 安徽師大中文系   Peking: Renmin wenxue chubanshe
人民文學出版社 , 1978.

Lu Ji 陸機. *Wenfu* 文賦 . In *Lu Shiheng ji* 陸士衡集 (*Sibu beiyao*).

Luo Binwang 駱賓王 . *Lu Cheng ji* 駱丞集 (*Congshu jicheng* 叢書集成).

Qian Zhongshu 錢鍾書 , ed. *Song shi xuanzhu* 宋詩選注 . Peking: Renmin
wenxue chubanshe, 1958.

Qu Wanli 屈萬里 . *Shijing shiyi* 詩經釋義 . Taibei: Huagang chubanshe
華岡出版社 , 1953.

Su Shi 蘇軾 . *Dongpo ji* 東坡集 (*Sibu Beiyao*).

119

Tao Qian 陶潛 . *Jingjie xiansheng ji* 靖節先生集 *(Sibu beiyao)*.

Wang Anshi 王安石 . *Linchuan xiansheng wenji* 臨川先生文集 . Shanghai: Zhonghua shuju, 1959.

Wang Shizhen 王士禎 . *Daijingtang shihua* 帶經堂詩話 . 1760, rep. Shanghai, n.d.

Wang Wei 王維 . *Wang Youcheng ji zhu* 王右丞集注 . Edited by Zhao Diancheng 趙殿成 *(Sibu beiyao)*.

Xie Tiao 謝朓 . *Xie Xuancheng ji jiaozhu* 謝宣城集校注 . Edited by Hong Shunlong 洪順隆 . Taibei: Zhonghua shuju, 1969.

Xie Zhen 謝榛 . *Siming shihua* 四溟詩話 . In Ding Fubao, ed., *Xu lidai shihua* 丁福保，續歷代詩話 .

Yan Yu 嚴羽 . *Canglang shihua* 滄浪詩話 . In He Wenhuan, ed., *Lidai shihua*.

Ye Xie 葉燮 . *Yuan shi* 原詩 . In Ding Fubao, ed., *Qing shihua* 清詩話 .

Yü Shouzhen 喻守眞 , ed. *Tang shi sanbaishou xiangxi* 唐詩三百首詳析 . Hong Kong: Zhonghua shuju, 1959.

Zhao Yi 趙翼 . *Oubei shihua* 甌北詩話 . Peking: Denmin wenxue chubanshe, 1963.

B. Works in Western Languages

Abrams, M. H. *The Mirror and the Lamp*. New York: Oxford University Press, 1958.

Aldridge, A. Owen. "East-West Relations: Universal Literature, Yes; Common Poetics, No," *Tamkang Review*, 10, Nos. 1 and 2 (1979), 17–33.

Alston, William P. *Philosophy of Language*. Englewood Cliffs, N.J.: Prentice-Hall, 1964.

Apollinaire, Guillaume. *Alcools*. Paris, Éditions de la Nouvelle Revue Française, 1920.

Austín, J. L. *How to Do Things with Words*. New York: Oxford University Press, 1962.

Benjamin, Walter. *Illuminations*. Ed. with an introduction, Hannah Arendt. Trans. Harry Zohn. New York: Harcourt, Brace, and World, 1968.

Birch, Cyril, ed. *An Anthology of Chinese Literature*. Vol. I. New York: Grove Press, 1965.

Collingwood, R. G. *The Principles of Art*. Oxford: Clarendon Press, 1938.

Cooper, Arthur, trans. *Li Po and Tu Fu*. Harmondsworth, Middlesex, England: Penguin Books, 1971.

Croce, Benedetto. *Aesthetics as Science of Expression and General Linguistic*. Trans. Douglas Ainslie. London: Macmillan and Co., 1929.

Davis, A. R. *Tu Fu*. New York: Twayne Publishers, 1971.

Dewey, John. *Art as Experience*. New York: Minton, Balch and Co., 1934.

Dickinson, Emily. *The Poems of Emily Dickinson*. Ed. Thomas H. Johnson. Cambridge, Mass.: The Belknap Press of Harvard University Press, 1955.

Dufrenne, Mikel. *Le Poétique*. Paris: Presses Universitaires de France, 1963.

——. *Language and Philosophy*. Trans. H. B. Veatch. Bloomington: Indiana University Press, 1963.

——. *Phénoménologie de l'expérience esthétique*. 2d ed. Paris: Presses

Universitaires de France, 1967. *The Phenomenology of Aesthetic Experience*. Trans. Edward S. Casey et al. Evanston: Northwestern University Press, 1973.

Eliot, T. S. *Notes Towards the Definition of Culture*. New York: Harcourt, Brace, 1949.

Ellis, John M. *The Theory of Literary Criticism: A Logical Analysis*. Berkeley, Los Angeles and London: University of California Press, 1974.

Eoyang, Eugene. "The Tone of the Poet and the Tone of the Translator." *Yearbook of Comparative and General Literature*, No. 24 (1975), 75–83.

Erlich, Victor. "Limits of the Biographical Approach." *Comparative Literature*, 6 (1954), 130–37.

Fang, Achilles. "Some Reflections on the Difficulty of Translation." In Reuben A. Brower, ed., *On Translation*. Cambridge, Mass.: Harvard University Press, 1959.

Fish, Stanley E. "How Ordinary is Ordinary Language?" *New Literary History*, 5, No. 1 (1973), 41–54.

———. "What is Stylistics and Why Are They Saying Such Terrible Things About It?" In Seymour Chatman, ed., *Approaches to Poetics*. New York and London: Columbia University Press, 1973.

Fokkema, D. W. "Cultural Relativism and Comparative Literature," *Tamkang Review*, 3, No. 2 (1972), 59–71.

———. "Chinese and Renaissance Artes Poeticae." *Comparative Literature Studies*, 15, No. 2 (1978), 159–65.

———. Rev. of *Chinese Theories of Literature* by James J. Y. Liu. *Dutch Quarterly Review of Anglo-American Letters*, 8 (1978), 157–59.

———. "New Strategies in the Comparative Study of Literature and Their Application to Contemporary Chinese Literature," in William Tay, Ying-hsiung Chou, and Heh-hsiang Yuan, eds., *China and the West: Comparative Literature Studies*. Hong Kong: The Chinese University Press, 1980.

Frankel, Hans H. "Yüeh-fu poetry." In Cyril Birch, ed., *Studies in Chinese Literary Genres*. Berkeley, Los Angeles and London: University of California Press, 1974.

———. *The Flowering Plum and the Palace Lady*. New Haven and London: Yale University Press, 1976.

Frodsham, J. D. *New Perspectives in Chinese Literature*. Canberra: Australian National University Press, 1970.

Frye, Northrop. *Anatomy of Criticism*. Princeton: Princeton University Press, 1957. Rpt. New York: Atheneum, 1970.

Graham, A. C., trans. *Poems of the Late T'ang*. Harmondsworth, Middlesex, England: Penguin Books, 1965.

———. " 'Being' in Classical Chinese." In John W. M. Verhaar, ed., *The Verb "Be" and Its Synonyms*. Dordrecht: D. Reidel, 1967.

Hawkes, David. *A Little Primer of Tu Fu*. Oxford: Clarendon Press, 1967.

———. Rev. of *Chinese Rhyme-prose* by Burton Watson. *Asia Major*, 18, pt. 2 (1973), 253.

Hightower, James R. "The *Wen Hsüan* and Genre Theory." *Harvard Journal of Asiatic Studies*, 20, Nos. 3–4 (1957), 512–33.

———, trans. *The Poetry of T'ao Ch'ien*. Oxford: Clarendon Press, 1970.

Hirsch, E. D., Jr. *Validity in Interpretation*. New Haven and London: Yale University Press, 1967.

————. *The Aims of Interpretation*. Chicago: University of Chicago Press, 1976.

Hung, William. *Tu Fu: China's Greatest Poet*. Cambridge, Mass.: Harvard University Press, 1952.

Husserl, Edmund. *Logical Investigations*. Trans. J. N. Finlay. New York: Humanities Press, 1970.

Ingarden, Roman. *The Literary Work of Art*. Trans. George G. Grabowicz. Evanston: Northwestern University Press, 1973.

————. *The Cognition of the Literary Work of Art*. Trans. Ruth Ann Crowley and Kenneth R. Olson. Evanston: Northwestern University Press, 1973.

————. "Artistic and Aesthetic Values." In Harold Osborne, ed., *Aesthetics*. London: Oxford University Press, 1972.

Iser, Wolfgang. "The Reading Process: A Phenomenological Approach." *New Literary History*, 3, No. 2 (1972), 279–99. Rpt. in his *The Implied Reader*. Baltimore and London: Johns Hopkins University Press, 1974.

————. *The Act of Reading*. Baltimore and London: Johns Hopkins University Press, 1978.

Jakobson, Roman. "Linguistics and Poetics." In Thomas A. Sebeok, ed., *Style in Language*. Cambridge, Mass.: MIT Press, 1960.

Jauss, Hans Robert. "The Alterity and Modernity of Medieval Literature." *New Literary History*, 10, No. 2 (1979), 181–227.

Kao, Yu-kung, and Tsu-lin Mei. "Syntax, Diction, and Imagery in T'ang Poetry." *Harvard Journal of Asiatic Studies*, 31 (1971), 49–135.

Karlgren, Bernhard, trans. *The Book of Odes*. Stockholm: Museum of Far Eastern Antiquities, 1974.

Kierkegaard, Søren, *Either/Or*. Trans. D. F. and L. M. Swenson. London: Oxford University Press, 1946.

Lefevere, André. "Some Tactical Steps Toward a Common Poetics." In William Tay, Ying-hsiung Chou, and Heh-hsiang Yuan, eds., *China and the West: Comparative Literature Studies*. Hong Kong: The Chinese University Press, 1980.

Levin, Samuel. "Concerning What Kind of Speech Act a Poem Is." In T. A. Van Dijk, ed., *Pragmatics of Language and Literature*. Amsterdam: North-Holland Publishing Co., 1976.

Lin, Shuen-fu. *The Transformation of the Chinese Lyrical Tradition: Chiang K'uei and Southern Sung Tz'u Poetry*. Princeton: Princeton University Press, 1978.

Liu, James J. Y. *Elizabethan and Yuan*. London: China Society, 1955.

————. *The Art of Chinese Poetry*. London: Routledge and Kegan Paul; Chicago: University of Chicago Press, 1962. Phoenix Books ed., University of Chicago Press, 1966; 4th impression, 1974.

————. "Towards a Chinese Theory of Poetry." *Yearbook of Comparative and General Literature*, No. 15 (1966), 159–65.

————. *The Chinese Knight-Errant*. London: Routledge and Kegan Paul; Chicago: University of Chicago Press, 1967.

————. *The Poetry of Li Shang-yin*. Chicago: University of Chicago Press, 1969.

————. *Major Lyricists of the Northern Sung*. Princeton: Princeton University Press, 1974.

———. "Polarity of Aims and Methods: Naturalization or Barbarization?" *Yearbook of Comparative and General Literature*, No. 24 (1975), 60–68.

———. *Chinese Theories of Literature*. Chicago: University of Chicago Press, 1975. Phoenix Books ed., 1979.

———. "The Study of Chinese Literature in the West: Recent Developments, Current Trends, Future Prospects." *Journal of Asian Studies*, 35, No. 1 (1975), 21–30.

———. "Language—Literature—Translation: A Bifocal Approach in a Tetradic Framework." In T. C. Lai, ed., *The Art and Profession of Translation*. Hong Kong: Hong Kong Translation Society, n.d.

———. "Towards a Synthesis of Chinese and Western Theories of Literature." *Journal of Chinese Philosophy*, 4 (1977), 1–24.

———. *Essentials of Chinese Literary Art*. North Scituate, Mass.: Duxbury Press, 1979.

———. "Time, Space, and Self in Chinese Poetry." *Chinese Literature: Essays, Articles, Reviews*, 1, No. 2 (1979), 137–56.

Liu, Wu-chi, and Irving Yucheng Lo, eds. *Sunflower Splendor*. Bloomington: Indiana University Press; New York: Anchor Press/Doubleday, 1975.

Magliola, Robert. *Phenomenology and Literature*. W. Lafayette: Purdue University Press, 1977.

Maritain, Jacques. *Creative Intuition in Art and Poetry*. New York: Pantheon Books, 1953.

Ohmann, Richard. "Speech Acts and the Definition of Literature." *Philosophy and Rhetoric*, 4 (1971).

———. "Literature as Act." In Seymour Chatman, ed. *Approaches to Poetics*. New York and London: Columbia University Press, 1973.

Owen, Stephen. *The Poetry of Meng Chiao and Han Yü*. New Haven and London: Yale University Press, 1975.

Pearce, Roy Harvey. *Historicism Once More*. Princeton: Princeton University Press, 1969.

Poulet, Georges. "Phenomenology of Reading." *New Literary History*, 1, No. 1 (1969), 53–68.

Pratt, Mary Louise. *Toward a Speech Act Theory of Literary Discourse*. Bloomington: Indiana University Press, 1977.

Quiller-Couch, Sir Arthur, ed. *The Oxford Book of English Verse*. Oxford: Clarendon Press, 1939.

Ricoeur, Paul. "The Model of the Text." *New Literary History*, 5, No. 1 (1973), 91–117.

———. *The Conflict of Interpretations*. Evanston: Northwestern University Press, 1974.

———. *Interpretation Theory*. Fort Worth: Texas Christian University Press, 1976.

Sartre, Jean-Paul. *Psychology of Imagination*. New York: Philosophical Library, 1948.

Searle, John R. *Speech Acts: An Essay in the Philosophy of Language*. London: Cambridge University Press, 1969.

Selver, Paul. *The Art of Translating Poetry*. Boston: The Writer, Inc., 1966.

Steiner, George. *Language and Silence*. New York: Atheneum, 1967.

———. *After Babel*. New York: Oxford University Press, 1975.

————. "Critic/Reader." *New Literary History*, 10, No. 3 (1979), 423–52.

Szondi, Peter. "Introduction to Literary Hermeneutics." *New Literary History*, 10, No. 1 (1978), 17–29.

Todorov, Tzvetan. "The Notion of Literature." *New Literary History*, 5, No. 1 (1973), 5–16.

Traugott, Elizabeth Closs. "On the Expression of Spatio-temporal Relations in Language." In Joseph H. Greenberg, Charles A. Ferguson, and Edith A. Moravcsik, eds., *Universals of Human Language*, Vol. III. Stanford: Stanford University Press, 1978.

Waley, Arthur. *The Poetry and Career of Li Po*. London: Allen and Unwin, 1950.

Walls, Jan W. "The Craft of Translating Poetic Structures and Patterns: Fidelity to Form." *Yearbook of Comparative and General Literature*, No. 24 (1975), 68–75.

Watson, Burton, trans. *Su Tung-p'o: Selections from a Sung Dynasty Poet*. New York and London: Columbia University Press, 1965.

————. *Chinese Lyricism: Shih Poetry from the Second to the Twelfth Century*. New York and London: Columbia University Press, 1971.

Wellek, René. *Concepts of Criticism*. New Haven and London: Yale University Press, 1963.

Wellek, René, and Austin Warren. *Theory of Literature*. 3d ed. New York: Harcourt, Brace, and World, 1962.

Wimsatt, W. K., Jr. *The Verbal Icon*. Lexington: University of Kentucky Press, 1967.

Yip, Wai-lim. *Chinese Poetry: Major Modes and Genres*. Berkeley, Los Angeles, and London: University of California Press, 1976.

List of Chinese Words and Names

Beida (Peita) 北大
Beijing Daxue (Pei-ching Ta-hsüeh) 北京大學
Cao Cao (Ts'ao Ts'ao) 曹操
cheng (ch'eng) 城
chi (ch'ih) 尺
Chijiao Daxian (Ch'ih-chiao Ta-hsien) 赤脚大仙
ci (tz'u) 詞
ci ri (tz'u jih) 此日
cipu (tz'u-p'u) 詞譜
Cui Hao (Ts'ui Hao) 崔顥
cunzai (ts'un-tsai) 存在
Du Fu (Tu Fu) 杜甫
fengwei (feng-wei) 風味
fu (fu) 賦
Gongan (Kung-an) 公安
gu wei jin yong, yang wei Zhong yong (ku wei chin yung, yang wei Chung yung) 古爲今用洋爲中體用
guti shi (ku-t'i shih) 古體詩
Han (Han) 漢
Han Yu (Han Yü) 韓愈
He Zhu (Ho Chu) 賀鑄
hou (hou) 後
huaigu shi (huai-ku shih) 懷古詩
Huang Tingjian (Huang T'ing-chien) 黃庭堅
Huangfu Shi (Huang-fu Shih) 皇甫湜
huigu (hui-ku) 回顧
huixiang (hui-hsiang) 回想
huiyi (hui-i) 回憶

125

Jian'an *ti* (Chien-an *t'i*) 建安體
Jiang Kui (Chiang K'uei) 姜夔
jin ri (*chin jih*) 今日
jing (*ching*) 景
jingjie (*ching-chieh*) 境界
jinti shi (*chin-t'i shih*) 近體詩
Jiubian (*Chiu-pien*) 九辯
jueju (*chüeh-chü*) 絶句
junzi (*chün-tzu*) 君子
Li Bi (Li Pi) 李璧
Li Bo (Li Po) or Li Bai (Li Pai) 李白
Li He (Li Ho) 李賀
Li Shangyin (Li Shang-yin) 李商隱
Liuzhi (Liu-chih) 柳枝
Lu Hongzhi (Lu Hung-chih) 盧弘止
Lu Ji (Lu Chi) 陸機
Ouyang Xiu (Ou-yang Hsiu) 歐陽修
qian (*ch'ien*) 前
Qian Zhongshu (Ch'ien Chung-shu) 錢鍾書
qiancheng (*ch'ien-ch'eng*) 前程
qianzhan (*ch'ien-chan*) 前瞻
qie (*ch'ieh*) 妾
qing (*ch'ing*) 情
qixiang (*ch'i-hsiang*) 氣象
qizhong ganku (*ch'i-chung kan-k'u*) 其中甘苦
qu (*ch'ü*) 曲
qunian (*ch'ü-nien*) 去年
shan (*shan*) 山
shan shang ren (*shan shang jen*) 山上人
Shen Deqian (Shen Te-ch'ien) 沈德潛
Shen Yue (Shen Yüeh) 沈約
shenyun (*shen-yün*) 神韻
shi (*shih*) (poetry) 詩
shi (*shih*) (be) 是
shi (*shih*) (event) 事
Shijing (*Shih-ching*) 詩經
shunü (*shu-nü*) 淑女
Sima Xiangru (Ssu-ma Hsiang-ju) 司馬相如
Song (Sung) 宋
Song shi xuanzhu (*Sung shih hsüan-chu*) 宋詩選注
Su Shi (Su Shih) 蘇軾
Taibo *ti* (T'ai-po *t'i*) 太白體
Tang (T'ang) 唐
ti (*t'i*) 體
timian (*t'i-mien*) 體面

Wang Anshi (Wang An-shih) 王安石
Wang Fuzhi (Wang Fu-chih) 王夫之
Wang Guowei (Wang Kuo-wei) 王國維
Wang Shizhen (Wang Shih-chen) 王士禛
Wang Wei (Wang Wei) 王維
Wangshu (Wang-shu) 望舒
wo (wo) 我
wu (wu) 物
wuhua (wu-hua) 物化
Wuning (Wu-ning) 武寧
xi shi (hsi shih) 昔時
xianglian ti (hsiang-lien t'i) 香奩體
Xianzhong (Hsien-chung) 顯忠
Xie Shang (Hsieh Shang) 謝尚
Xie Tiao (Hsieh T'iao) 謝朓
Xie Zhen (Hsieh Chen) 謝榛
Xikun *ti* (Hsi-k'un *t'i*) 西崑體
xuemo (hsüeh-mo) 血脈
Yan Yu (Yen Yü) 嚴羽
Ye Xie (Yeh Hsieh) 葉燮
yinyi (yin-i) 隱逸
yongshi shi (yung-shih shih) 詠史詩
yongwu shi (yung-wu shih) 詠物詩
you (yu) 有
youxia (yu-hsia) 游俠
Yuan Hong (Yuan Hung) 袁宏
Yuan Hongdao (Yuan Hung-tao) 袁宏道
Yuan Zhongdao (Yuan Chung-tao) 袁中道
Yuan Zongdao (Yuan Tsung-tao) 袁宗道
yuanyang (yuan-yang) 鴛鴦
yuefu (yüeh-fu) 樂府
yundu (yün-tu) 韻度
yunsheng (yün-sheng) 韻聲
Zhao Yi (Chao I) 趙翼
zhiji (chih-chi) 知己
Zhou (Chou) 周
Zhuangzi (Chuang Tzu) 莊子

INDEX

Abrams, M. H., 5, 73
Adonis, 6
Aims of Interpretation, The, 57
Aldridge, A. Owen, 105–107
Analects of Confucius, The, xii
Apollinaire, Guillaume, 80
applicatio, 57
Ariel, 6
Aristotle, 2
Art of Chinese Poetry, The, xvi
Auerbach, Erich, 52
Austin, J. L., 2
Ayling, Alan, 40

Ba Mountain, 80
Barrett, Elizabeth (Browning), 2
Beida (Beijing Daxue), xiv
Benjamin, Walter, 40
Bible, 40, 50
Blake, William, xiv, 20
Book of Poetry, The (Shijing), 19, 28–30, 48
Book of Snobs, The, xiii
Bowra, Sir (Cecil) Maurice, xv
Bristol, University of, xiv
British Council, xiv
Brontë, Emily, 2
Brooks, Cleanth, 107
Browning, Robert, 2, 40
Bynner, Witter, 38

Camus, Albert, 50
Cao Cao, 48

Chang'an, 28
Chang'e, 41
Chapman, George, 40
Chaucer, Geoffrey, xiv
Chaves, Jonathan, 38
Chen Zi'ang, 83
cheng ("city wall"), 19
chi (Chinese "foot"), 59
Chicago, University of, xv
Ch'ien Chung-shu, 71
Chijiao Daxian, 18
Chinese Theories of Literature, xvii
ci ("lyric"), xi, 34, 63, 73
cipu (manual on lyric metres), 63
Clemen, W. H., 55
Coleridge, S. T., 22, 55
Collingwood, R. G., xvi, 5, 68
Confucius, 52, 53
Conrad, Joseph, xii
Copperfield, David, 6
corrigible schemata, 61
creativity, 69
Croce, Benedetto, 34
Cui Hao, 32, 99
cultural relativism, 54, 65–66

da Vinci, Leonardo, 10
Dante, 50, 59
Dewey, John, 10
Diana (goddess of the moon), 41
Dickens, Charles, xiii
Dickinson, Emily, 60, 87
Doctrine of the Mean, The, xii

Donne, John, xiv
Dostoevsky, Fedor, xiii
Dream of the Red Chamber, 50
Dryden, John, 40
Du Fu, 19, 22, 24–27, 31, 43, 59, 61–63, 69, 92–94, 97, 100–102
Dufrenne, Mikel, xvi, xvii, 5, 7, 8, 67

Ecke, Gustav, xiv
Eliot, T. S., xiv, xvi, 59, 69
Ellis, John M., 17
Elizabethan and Yuan, xv
Empson, William, xiv, xvi
Erlich, Victor, 73
Etièmble, René, 105
Eurocentrism, 51, 53, 54, 65

fengwei ("flavor"), 8
FitzGerald, Edward, 40
Fokkema, D. W., 51, 54, 55, 65–66, 105
Four Books, The, xii
Frankel, Hans, 38, 101
Freud, Sigmund, 50, 51, 54, 59, 60
Frizer, Ingram, xii
Frodsham, J. D., 54
Frye, Northrop, 15
fu ("rhymeprose"), xiii
Fu Jen University, xiii

Giles, H. A., 40
Goethe, J. W. von, 50, 55
Gongan School, 70
Gorky, Maxim, xiii
Graham, A. C., 38
Great Learning, The, xii
guti shi ("Ancient Style Poetry"), 33, 79

Hamlet, 7
Hamlet, 55, 68
Han Yu, 9, 69, 81–82
Hardy, Thomas, xiii
Hawaii, University of, xv
Hawkes, David, 38, 41, 101
He Zhizhang, 89
He Zhu, 71
Heidegger, Martin, xvii
Henry VIII, 6
hermeneutical circle, 4, 53, 61
hermeneutical spiral, 61–63
Hightower, J. R., 88
Hillary, Sir Edmund, 10
Hirsch, E. D., Jr., 12, 33, 54, 57, 61, 65, 75
historical relativism, 52, 54–55, 65
historicism, 51–53, 65
Homer, 6, 50
Hong Kong, Chinese University of, xv
Hong Kong, University of, xv

Horace, 73
Hotson, Leslie, xii
huaigu shi ("poems recalling antiquity"), 33
Huang Tingjian, 69
Huangfu Shi, 9
Huis Clos, 55
Husserl, Edmund, xvi, 21, 22

Ibsen, Henrik, 50
Ingarden, Roman, xvi, xvii, 5–7, 10, 14–15, 20, 47, 66
interpretatio, 57
Iser, Wolfgang, 20, 21

James, Henry, xii, xv
Jauss, Hans Robert, 56
Jian'an ti ("Jian'an style"), 33
Jiang Kui, 7, 8, 32
jing ("scene"), xvii, 9
Jing Ke, 90, 95
jingjie ("world"), 5, 6, 7
Jingmen, 100–101
Jingting Mountain, 45–46
jinti shi ("Recent Style poetry"), 33
Jiubian ("Nine Arguments"), 92
jueju. See Quatrain
Joseph, Bertram M., xiv
Juliet, 47
Julius Caesar, xiv, 6
junzi ("young lord"), 41

Kant, Immanuel, 65
Karlgren, Bernhard, 38
King Lear, 69
Knight, G. Wilson, xvi
Kott, Jan, 55

Laertes, 68
Lefevere, André, 105
Legge, James, 40
Lenin, 50
Li Bi, 71
Li Bo, 27–28, 31, 35–36, 45, 79–80, 96–97, 102–103
Li He, 9, 58, 91
Li Shangyin, 23–24, 31–32, 34, 53, 59, 60, 73, 80–81
Lin, Shuen-fu, 32
Liuzhi (Willow Branch), 31–32
Lo, Irving, 43, 101
London, University of, xv
Lowell, Amy, 38
Lu Hongzhi, 24
Lu Ji, 8, 9, 108
Luo Binwang, 95

Macbeth, 6, 80

Mackintosh, Duncan, 40
MacLeish, Archibald, 10
Mallarmé, Stéphane, xvi
Mansfield, Katherine, xiv
Mao Zedong, 50
Maritain, Jacques, 6
Marvell, Andrew, 86
Marlowe, Christopher, xii, xiv, 6
Marx, Karl, 50, 51
meaning, 12, 20–22, 57, 59
Mencius, The Book of, xii
Merleau-Ponty, Maurice, xvi
Milton, John, 19
Ming Fei, 100–102
Mona Lisa, 10
Moore, Marianne, 40
Morozov, M. M., 55
Mrs. Dalloway, xiv

New Asia College, xv
noema, xvii
noesis, xvii
Ophelia, 7
originality, 68–73
Orlando, xiv
Ouyang Xiu, 73–74
Owen, Stephen, 38, 82
Oxford University, xv

Pannwitz, Rudolph, 40
Pearce, Roy Harvey, 53
Pengzu, 91
perspectivism, 52, 55
phenomenology, xvii, 21
Piaget, Jean, 61
Pittsburgh, University of, xv
Pope, Alexander, 40
Poulet, Georges, 20
Pound, Ezra, 38, 52
Pushkin, Alexander, 73

Qian Zhongshu, 71
qing ("feeling" or "emotion"), xvii, 9
qixiang ("atmosphere"), 7
qu (dramatic poetry), xi
Quatrain (*jueju*), xiii, 35, 74
Queen Mother of the West, 91

Red Mansion Dream, A, 56, 60
Rexroth, Kenneth, 38
Richard II, 6
Richards, I. A., xvi
Ricoeur, Paul, 11, 20, 56, 61, 103
Rimbaud, Arthur, xviii
roman à clef, 60
Romeo, 47
Rossetti, Christina, 81

Saint George, 6
Sartre, Jean-Paul, 7, 55
Schlegel, A. W., 55
School of Oriental and African Studies, xv
Seven Types of Ambiguity, xiv
Shakespeare, William, xiv, xv, 6, 13, 20, 31, 55, 60, 69, 82
Shen Deqian, 35
Shen Yue, 72
shenyun ("spirit and tone"), 8
shi ("poetry"), xi, 77
shi ("event"), 9
significance, 12, 57, 59
Sima Xiangru, 59
sincerity, 68, 73–74
Sinocentrism, 51, 52–53, 65
Snyder, Gary, 38
Songshi xuanzhu, 71
Song Yu, 92
Sonnets from the Portuguese, 2
Southampton, Earl of, 13
Stanford University, xv
Steiner, George, xi, 76
"Stone-moat Village Officer," 25–27, 43
Story of the Stone, The, 50
Su Duan, 62–63
Su Shi, 34, 84–86
Symonds, J. A., 40
Szondi, Peter, 51

Taibo ti (Li Bo's style), 33
Tale of Genji, The, 50
Tao, xvii
Tao Qian, 86–88, 90, 95
Taoism, xvii
Taste, 67–68
tastes, 67–68
Thackeray, W. M., xiii
ti ("genre" or "style"), 33
Tianwu, 91
timian ("countenance"), 7
Timur, 6
To the Lighthouse, xiv
Tolstoy, Leo, xiii, 50
transculturism, 55–56, 64, 66, 105
transhistoricism, 55–56, 64, 66, 105
Tsing Hua University, xiv
Turgenev, Ivan, xiii

Validity in Interpretation, 57
Vaughan, Henry, 83
Vergil, 19
Voltaire, 6
Wadham College, xiv
Waley, Arthur, 38, 40
Wallenstein, 6
Wang Anshi, 71

Wang Fuzhi, xvi
Wang Guowei, xvi, 5, 6, 7
Wang Qiang (Wang Zhaojun), 101
Wang Shizhen, xvi, 8
Wang Wei, 2, 44, 46, 71–72, 74, 97–98
Wangshu, 81
Watson, Burton, 38, 46, 48
Wellek, René, xvi, xvii, 52–53, 55, 56, 65, 66
wen ("literature"), 107
Wilde, Oscar, xiii, xiv
Wimsatt, W. K., Jr., xvi, 12
wo ("subject"), xvii
wo cunzi ("I exist"), xviii
wo shi ("I am"), xviii
Woolf, Virginia, xii, xiv
wu ("object"), xvii
Wuning, 24
Wuxian, 91

Xianzhong, Monk, 71–72, 74
xianglian ti ("style of boudoir verse"), 34
Xie Shang, 96
Xie Tiao, 35
Xie Tiao's Pavilion, 79
Xie Zhen, 9
Xihe, 81
Xikun ti ("style of the Xikun School"), 34
Xuanzhou, 79

Xue Fu, 62–63
Xue Hua, 62
xuemuo ("veins"), 7

Yan, Prince Dan of, 90, 95
Yan Yu, xvi, 7
Ye Xie, 9
Yellow Crane Tower, 98–99
Yellow River, 102–103
yinyi ("recluse"), 94
Yip, Wai-lim, 42
yongshi shi ("poems on history"), 90
yongwu shi ("poems on objects"), 33
Youzhou, 83
Yuan Hong, 96
Yuan Hongdao, 70
Yuan Zhongdao, 70
Yuan Zongdao, 70
yuanyang ("mandarin duck"), 46
yuefu ("Music Department songs"), 35
Yuguan (Jade Pass), 28
Yujie yuan ("Grievance on the Marble Steps"), 35–36
yundu ("tone"), 7
yunsheng ("tone"), 8

Zhao Yi, 69
zhiji ("one who appreciates you"), 90
Zhongnan, 97
Zhou (dynasty), 59
Zhuangzi, 86–87, 88